Mount Edgcumbe

Mount Edgcumbe
by
Derek Tait

Driftwood Coast Publishing

Frontispiece : The Avenue at the beginning of the 1900s.

First published 2009

Driftwood Coast Publishing
PO Box 7,West Park,Plymouth,PL5 2YS.
© Derek Tait, 2009

Price £9.99.

Contents

Acknowledgements

Photo credits : The Earl of Mount Edgcumbe Collection, Steve Johnson, The Driftwood Coast Photo Library, Derek Tait and Tina Cole.
Thanks also to The Earl of Mount Edgcumbe, Kate Johnson, Wendy Penwill and Ian Berry for all their help.
I have tried to track down the copyright holders of all photos used and apologise to anyone who hasn't been mentioned.
Check out my website at www.derektait.co.uk and my local history blog at http://plymouthlocalhistory.blogspot.com

Bibliography

Books:

A Complete Parochial History of the County (Published in 1870).
A guide to the coasts of Devon and Cornwall (Published in 1859).
A Londoner's Walk to the Land's End and a trip to the Scilly Isles by Walter White (Published in 1879).
An Authentic Narrative of the Death of Lord Nelson by Sir William Beatty (Published in 1807).
A select collection of poems with notes by J. Nichols (Published in 1780).
Animals Graves and Memorials by Jan Toms (Shire Publications 2006).
An Anecdote Biography by John Timbs (Published in 1860).
Black's Guide to Devonshire (Published in 1864).
Census of Cornwall (Published 1891).
Cornwall by Arthur Leslie Salmon (Published 1903).
Cornwall and the Isles of Scilly : the complete guide by David Clegg (Published in 2005).
History of Plymouth and Her Neighbours by C W Bracken (Underhill 1931).
Images of England : Plymouth by Derek Tait (Tempus 2003).
Journal of a Tour around the Southern coasts of England by John Henry Manners (Published in 1805).
Journal of the British Archaeological Association (Published in 1887).
Lake's Parochial History of the County of Cornwall by Joseph Polsue (Published 1868).
Letter of Harriet, Countess of Granville, written in 1815 to Lady G Morpeth.
Lord Byron and some of his Contemporaries by Leigh Hunt (Published in 1828).

More Famous Homes of Great Britain and their stories by Alfred Henry Malan (Published in 1902).

Mount Edgcumbe House and Country Park: A Guide by Cynthia Gaskell Brown (Mount Edgcumbe Country Park 2003).

Neolithic Enclosures in Atlantic Northwest Europe by Timothy Darvill and Julian Thomas (Published in 2001).

Nettleton's Guide of 1829.

Pall Mall Magazine (Published in 1897).

Passages from the Diaries of Mrs Philip Lybbe Powys of Hardwick House, Oxon: A.D. 1756-1808 (Published in 1899).

Plymouth A New History by Crispin Gill (David Charles 1966).

Plymouth at War by Derek Tait (Tempus 2006).

Plymouth Pictures from the Past by Guy Fleming (Devon Books 1995).

Secret Memoirs Of The Courts Of Europe Vol I by Henry Swinburne (Published in 1840).

The Antiquarian and Topographical Cabinet (Published in 1809).

The Book of Fair Devon by the United Devon Association (Published in 1900).

The Bystander (Published in 1905).

The Devonshire and Cornwall Illustrated (Published in 1832).

The Directory of Plymouth, Stonehouse and Devonport by Robert Brindley (Published in 1830).

The Genealogy of the Existing British Peerage by Edmund Lodge (Published in 1838).

The Gentleman's Magazine (Published in 1853).

The Handbook for Travellers (Published in 1851).

The History of Cornwall by Fortescue Hitchins and Samuel Drew (Published in 1824).

The Literary Journal (Published in 1821).

The Monthly Review of 1813.

The National Archives for 25th May 1639.

The Quarterly Review of 1840.

The Plymouth and Devonport Guide : With Sketches of the Surrounding Scenery by Henry Edmund Carrington (Published in 1828).

The Ports, Harbours, Watering-places and Coast Scenery of Great Britain (Published 1842).

The Rame Register (1701).

The South Devon and South Cornwall Guide (Published 1908).

The Story of My Life : Marie Queen of Roumania (Published in 1934).

The Survey of Cornwall by Richard Carew (Published in 1602).

The Tourist's Guide to South Devon : Rail, Road, River and Moor (Published in 1883).

The United Service Magazine (Published in 1867).
The West Britton of 27 January 1817.
The West Briton Newspaper in the Quarter Century from 1810 to 1835.
The Works with Acopious Index (Published in 1823).
Travels through North America, during the years 1825 and 1826 by His Highness Bernhard, Duke of Saxe-Weimar Eisenach (Published in 1828).
Visitors' Guide to Mount Edgcumbe by Louis Duprez (Published in 1871.

Websites:

Brian Moseley's Plymouth Data website at www.plymouthdata.info
Historical Cornwall at http://www.historic-cornwall.org.uk/
Mount Edgcumbe House and Country Park at
http://www.mountedgcumbe.gov.uk/
Plymouth South Western Defences at
http://www.ecastles.co.uk/plymouthcentral.html
Public Monument and Sculpture Association at
http://pmsa.cch.kcl.ac.uk/BL/Region.htm
Steve Johnson's Cyberheritage website at http://www.cyber-heritage.co.uk
The Edgcumbe Arms at http://www.edgcumbearms.co.uk/history.html
The Friends of Mount Edgcumbe at http://www.fomecp.org.uk/

Newspapers
Evening Herald
Western Morning News

Driftwood Coast Publishing
© Derek Tait 2009

Introduction

In 1493, Sir Piers Edgcumbe married Joan Durnford and her dowry included land on both sides of the Tamar. In 1515, King Henry VIII granted Piers permission to empark deer on the land now known as Mount Edgcumbe and between 1547 and 1553, Sir Richard Edgcumbe of Cotehele added a new home to the deer park.

Adjacent to the house is the Earl's Garden which was laid out in the 18th Century. Contained in the garden are many ancient and rare trees including a Mexican Pine, a Lucombe Oak and a 400 year old Lime. At the far end of the garden is an ornamental shell seat.

The ornamental gardens near the Orangery were a wilderness garden during the 17th Century. However, during the 18th Century, the Italian, French and English gardens were laid out.

After his defeat, Napoleon requested that he be imprisoned at Mount Edgcumbe House but this request was denied and he was exiled to the Island of St Helena instead.

During the Victorian and Edwardian times, Mount Edgcumbe proved to be very popular and was visited by Royalty and the celebrities of the day. It was open to the public on every Monday. A Plymouth man, Sam Webber, would lease out boats from Stonehouse Creek to people for 6d an hour. The boats were between 12ft and 18ft and young couples would row over to Mount Edgcumbe for the day.

Mount Edgcumbe House, which was built of red stone, with a stucco finish, survived for hundreds of years until it was the victim of a direct hit during a German bomb attack in 1941. The outer walls remained but the interior had to be rebuilt and this work was completed in 1964. Unfortunately, many family records, historical documents, pictures and artefacts were lost forever. Ironically, during the war years, Adolf Hitler had shown an interest in living at Mount Edgcumbe if Germany won the war.

During 1944, the US Army (110th Field Artillery of the 29th Infantry Division) occupied the area around Barn Pool before leaving for Normandy to take part in the D-Day landings. Evidence of their time there can still be seen today and remnants of the 'hards', that their vehicles drove over, can be found scattered on the beach. Soldiers names can also be found carved into the trees nearby. After the war, Mount Edgcumbe Park was open to visitors on every Wednesday, on Bank Holidays and the last Saturday of the month.

When the Mount Edgcumbe estate was loaned paintings from the Lord Harmsworth collection, they showed the Italian Garden in all its original glory. The gardens are now laid out in the original style with elements such as the Agaves taken from one of the Nicholas Condy watercolours in the collection. Condy was a local artist who was born in Torpoint in 1793.

During 1971, the house and its grounds were sold to Cornwall County and Plymouth City Councils and the house was leased to the family. Mount Edgcumbe is indeed a beautiful place to visit and today, it remains much as it has for the last couple of hundred years.

Mount Edgcumbe Country Park has an area of 865 acres along with 10 miles of coastline.

Samuel Pepys, in 1683, described Mount Edgcumbe as 'a most beautiful place as ever was seen' .However, Dr. Johnson, referring to the view from Mount Edgecumbe, noted, 'though there is the grandeur of a fleet, there is also the impression of there being a dockyard, the circumstances of which are not agreeable.' It was thought that the town of Plymouth with its buildings and dockyard somehow spoiled the beautiful view.

If you're a regular visitor, like myself, I hope that this book will add to your knowledge of Mount Edgcumbe. However, if you're reading this book and you've never been there, please make sure that you go!

One

Cremyll

The Cremyll Ferry is said to have originated during Saxon times. It first appears in documentation in 1204, in the papers of Reginald de Valletort, and was one of the major crossing routes between Devon and Cornwall. The rights to the ferry were, at the time, granted to Ralph Edgcumbe and the family continued to lease them out until 1943 when the Millbrook Steamboat and Trading Company took over. It was then bought by the company from the Edgcumbe family in 1945.

The ferry originally left from a slipway at Devil's Point and landed on the Cremyll shore near to where the Passage House and Gardens once stood, on the spot where the Orangery now stands. The Passage House, the gardens and Schillhall Cottage were leased with the ferry rights until the Italian Garden was laid out in the 1700s. The landing place was then moved northwards.

A picture showing the ferry laden with passengers arriving at Cremyll. The tide is low and small boats take the passengers safely to land. Casks wait on the jetty possibly on their way to the Mount Edgcumbe Arms.

The Ferry journey could be a dangerous and trying one especially with the strong currents. Celia Fiennes, who lived at the same time as Daniel Defoe, wrote of her tour in 1698 between Plymouth and Penzance. She mentions the journey to Cremyll, which at the time was called ,'Crilby' :

'From Plymouth I went one mile to Crilby Ferry which is a very hazardous crossing passage by reason of three tides meeting. Had I known the danger before, I would not have been very willing to have gone it, not but this is the constant way most people go and saves several miles riding. I was at least an hour going over and it was about a mile, but indeed in some places, notwithstanding there were five men rowing and I set my own men to row also, I do believe that we made almost not a step of the way for a quarter of an hour, but blessed by God I came safely over; but those ferry boats are so wet and the sea is always so cold to be upon that I never fail to catch cold in a ferry boat as I did this day, having two more ferries to cross, tho' none so bad or half so long as this. Thence to Millbrook, 2 miles, and went all along by the water and had the full view of the dockyards.'

The Rame Register of 1701 reports that six women and a man were drowned at Crimble on the 26th July.

The fares for the ferry in 1810 were five shillings for a coach with four horses and a guinea for a hearse with a coffin.

Louis Duprez wrote, in his Visitors' Guide to Mount Edgcumbe, published in 1871, that, **'the beach is crowded with hundreds of visitors and boatmen are vociferating loudly in their zealous endeavour to embark as many fares as possible. There are gingerbread and sweetmeats stalls and trade is brisk at the Mount Edgcumbe Arms, an old fashioned well-regulated house.'**

In 1885, steam boats were introduced. These towed a horse boat which, on many occasions, broke loose and had to be recovered down river.

There has been a shipyard to the right of the Mount Edgcumbe Arms for hundreds of years. It was taken over by Mashfords in 1930 and during the Second World War, the company built assault landing craft and anti-submarine motor launches for the Admiralty. Mashfords have also had many famous customers including Sir Francis Chichester, Sir Alec Rose and Ann Davison who, at the age of 39, was the first woman to single-handedly sail the Atlantic. She left Plymouth on the 18th May, 1952 in the boat, The Felicity Ann, which was purpose-built by Mashford Brothers Ltd. Work commenced on the boat in 1939 but was delayed by the Second World War and it wasn't launched until 1949.

Stonehouse was once known as East Stonehouse to distinguish it from the hamlet of West Stonehouse which stood on the opposite side of the river, near to Cremyll, which was said to have been burnt down by the French in the 1350s. West Stonehouse was originally owned by the ancient family, the Valletorts, and was in turn passed by marriage to the Durnford family before finally being passed to the Edgcumbe family as the dowry of Joan Durnford when she married Sir Piers Edgcumbe in 1493.

Carew wrote in his Survey of Cornwall in 1602:

'Certaine old ruines yet remaining confirm the neighbours' report that near the water's side, there stood once a towne called West Stonehouse until the French by fire and sword overthrew it.'

This passage refers to the Breton raids of the late 1300s and early 1400s. However, in The Directory of Plymouth, Stonehouse and Devonport by Robert Brindley, published in 1830, he states:

'About 1730, Barnpool was removed for the annoyance which it caused to the lordly domain of Mount Edgcumbe, and at the same time, West Stonehouse which had a chapel and was inhabited by fishermen was razed by the owners of the lovely domain of Mount Edgcumbe and not destroyed by the French as generally supposed.'

The accounts contradict each other but it is probable that West Stonehouse was destroyed by the French and the place referred to in Brindley's Directory refers to the remains of the hamlet. These remains would have been cleared away when the formal gardens were laid out in the 1700s. The small chapel that was at Barn Pool was said to have been removed and placed in the Picklecombe Valley and formed part of Picklecombe Seat.

West Stonehouse, or its remains, were still in existence in 1515 when King Henry VIII granted Sir Piers Edgcumbe a royal licence to keep deer at 'Westonehouse and Cremele.'

In the Journal of the British Archaeological Association, published in 1887, the Earl of Mount Edgcumbe, who was President of the association, wrote an early history of the family. He mentions:

'By his first marriage, with Jane Durnford, some time within the last decade of the century, he acquired the estates of the Stonehouse family on both sides of the river-mouth. At East Stonehouse, which is still the legal name of the town, there was a manor-house at which he sometimes lived ; near the site of West Stonehouse, there was a village which was destroyed by the French in the fourteenth century, and of which every vestige, as well as its name, is lost.'

Many of these buildings are now gone in this early view of the site of today's Mashfords. Vessels and ships have been built and serviced in this area for over 270 years and the site was acquired by the Mashford Brothers in 1930.

A photo from the early 1900s showing passengers from the ferry. The horse and buggy wait at the top of the slipway. The man on the right of the picture is carrying a wicker basket with a cat inside.

A horse and cab waiting for passengers on the Cremyll side of the crossing. The Tower House in the background once housed a bell. It dates from the time of Ernest Augustus Edgcumbe and is Italianate in design.

Joshua Reynolds was said to have completed his first portrait at the age of 12 in a boat house at Cremyll in 1735. The story was told in 'An Anecdote Biography' By John Timbs in 1860. It makes interesting reading, not just for the connection between Reynolds and Cremyll but it also shows the friendship that existed between Reynolds and Richard Edgcumbe:

'Reynolds first portrait was painted when he could not have been more than twelve years old. It was the portrait of the Reverend Thomas Smart, in whose family the tradition is that in 1735, a young Joshua coloured the likeness in a boat-house at Cremyll beach under Mount Edgcumbe, on canvas which was part of a boat-sail, and with the common paint used by shipwrights. Mr Smart was the tutor in the family of Richard Edgcumbe, Esq, who afterwards became the first Lord Edgcumbe, the ' Dick Edgcumbe' of Walpole's correspondence ; and young Reynolds seems to have been passing the holidays at Mount Edgcumbe with one of his sons. The portrait is said to have been painted from a drawing taken in church, and on the artist's thumb-nail : Hogarth was wont to sketch in a similar manner. The picture was for many years at Mount Edgcumbe, but was afterwards sent to Plympton, and hung up in one of the rooms belonging to the Corporation, of which Mr. Smart was a member. It was subsequently returned to

Mount Edgcumbe, and given by the present Earl to Mr Boger, of Wolsdon, the descendant and representative of Mr Smart, by whom these circumstances were related to Mr Cotton. This portrait has been accurately engraved by S W Reynolds. Mr Boger has also a small portrait or panel of the daughter of Mr Smart, which is supposed to have been painted by Reynolds. At the above time, Mr Edgcumbe was one of the patrons of the Borough of Plympton, which accounts for the acquaintance between the boys. Young Richard Edgcumbe had also a good deal of taste for drawing, and some of his paintings are still at Mount Edgcumbe. He became one of Walpole's constant Christmas and Easter guests at Strawberry Hill ; and Reynolds, who painted the tutor on sail-cloth, in 1735, in his boyhood, likewise painted young Edgcumbe for Walpole, when he had reached the zenith of his fame, in a charming picture with Selwyn and Gilly Williams. Walpole describes this picture as by far one of the best things Reynolds had executed : it is engraved in Cunningham's edition of Walpole's Letters ; the original picture, a little larger than cabinet size, was bought by the Right Honorable Henry Labouchere, now Lord Taunton, at the Strawberry Hill sale, in 1842.

There is also at Mount Edgcumbe a portrait of Richard Lord Edgcumbe, painted by Sir Joshua when he was an untaught boy at Plympton, and before he went to London.'

Cremyll has had many different names over the years including Crimela (1201), Cremill (1512), Crilby (1698), Crimbel (1701) and later, Crimhill. Mount Edgcumbe Estate became a very popular destination for visitors during Victorian and Edwardian times. Steamboat trips would leave The Hoe and Waterside at Saltash laden with passengers including Sunday School teachers complete with picnic hampers. Others would row across from Stonehouse Creek and spend long Summer days exploring the park.

The slipway leading towards the Cremyll Ferry. The Italian Tower House in the background was destroyed by German bombing during April 1941. Mount Edgcumbe House also took a direct hit. On the 23rd April, firemen from the ARP reported that they had put a fire out in the roof of Mashfords boatyard but had to let the tower burn due to lack of water.

A photo showing the ferryman waiting for passengers from the Cremyll Ferry. In the background can be seen HMS Impregnable. Groups of sailors are gathered by the waterside preparing small gigs.

A group of girls, wearing straw hats, sit near to the harbour. In the Second World War, during the bombing of Cremyll in April 1941, three people lost their lives including the ferry skipper and engineer.

A close up of the ferryman waiting for passengers from Stonehouse. A soldier stands to the left and a sailor can be seen on the right. On the far left are several Naval vessels.

HMS Impregnable moored off Cremyll.

HMS Impregnable was moored off Cremyll until 1906. The wooden battleship was launched in 1860 and, apart from trials, it never went to sea. Over a period of 25 years, she sat in the Hamoaze before being used as a Naval training ship. Originally called 'Howe', she was renamed in 1885 and then became the 'Bulwark'. In 1886, her name was changed again, this time to 'Impregnable'. In 1906, she was joined by the 'Inconstant' and 'Black Prince' before being moved further up river.

This early photo from the Earl of Mount Edgcumbe collection shows HMS Impregnable and other Naval ships in the background. The Tower House can be seen on the left of the picture.

A very busy scene around the quay at Cremyll. A large crowd in the background wait for the ferry as a small yacht sails by. During Victorian and Edwardian times, Mount Edgcumbe became a very popular place to visit.

A picture of the School House at Cremyll. In 1891, the school mistress was a Mary Chubb, aged 70, who lived at Tower Cottage in Cremyll. She was widowed at the time and had two daughters, one of whom was married to a John Ferrars. She had three grandsons living with her at the time. Her eldest daughter, Mary Ann Leworthy, aged 48, was also a school mistress.

The clock by the landing jetty. The writing around the clock face reads, 'Time and Tide Tarry for None". The frame surrounding the clock reads, 'Dost thou love life? Then do not squander time'. The clock was presented by Colonel Edgcumbe in 1885.

The Edgcumbe Arms. The original building dates back to the 15th century and featured stone flagged floors and oak beams. Unfortunately, a fire in January 1995 left the building little more than a shell but it has now been rebuilt and restored to its former glory.

Two

The Avenue and the House

Below the house is the beautifully tree-lined Avenue leading up from Cremyll towards Mount Edgcumbe House. The trees consist of sycamore, sweet chestnut and horse chestnut. Many of the trees were lost in the great blizzard of 1891 which devastated areas of the estate including the beech plantation above Lady Emma's Cottage.

The Great Blizzard of March 1891 affected many parts of the country particularly the South West. The strong gales and heavy snowfall hit Cornwall, Devon, Dorset, Herefordshire and Kent. London was also hit by the strong winds and snowfalls. Some snow drifts were fifteen feet high.

The devastation left behind included uprooted trees and blown away fencing and roofs. The storms were so ferocious that much of Cornwall and Devon were cut off from the rest of Britain for four days between 9th and 13th March, 1891. In this time, over 200 people were killed as well as 6,000 animals.

A lovely photo from the Victorian period showing three ladies dressed in their Sunday best enjoying the delights of the tree-lined Avenue.

An early photo of the Avenue taken in Winter.

The Monthly Review of 1813 described the estate within its pages. It read:

'Mount Edgcumbe, near Plymouth, is the beautiful seat and park belonging to the Earl of Mount Edgcumbe. The public days for visiting this most enchanted spot are Mondays, Wednesdays and Fridays; the only ceremony required, being that of setting down your name and address in a book, kept for that purpose at the Porter's Lodge. You are then permitted to stroll through the park and grounds, which contain most delightful walks, particularly that which terminates with a view of Cawsand Bay. A cottage is built in the park for the accommodation of strangers, where hot water for making tea and other conveniences may be procured. Those who

make this pleasant excursion generally furnish themselves with a hamper of provisions. The vast number of parties in the summertime, from the adjacent town and country, for the purpose of visiting Mount Edgcumbe, gives the park the appearance of a fair being held. On the public days, numerous groups are assembled, some playing, some singing, some dancing, which forms a rural scene, highly exhilarating, from the number of well-dressed women, who give life to the different parties.
The walks and grounds from various points are supposed to possess the most complete views of hill, wood and water in England.'

A passage from Henry Swinburne's book, 'Secret Memoirs Of The Courts Of Europe Vol I' , published in 1840, mentions a trip to Mount Edgcumbe in its pages:
'Our next course took us across the Lavy at low water, and we rode through Plymouth, which is ill paved and ugly; thence two miles further on to Dock, on as bad a road as any in England; took boat at Malton Cove, crossed the Narrows, and landed near the low gate of Mount Edgcumbe. Avenues lead up to the house; a good approach, low gardens, charming views of the sea, shipping, fort and islands. The vegetation is surprising - such handsome evergreens, cypresses, magnolias, myrtles, all blooming in the

open air. The house is Gothic and ill constructed, with an ugly hall of Devonshire marble; but there Is no describing the grandeur of the prospects. There is a new road cut along the side of the hill towards the sea, through a wilderness of pines, arbutus, and other evergreens. Close to the park is Maker Church, from the steeple of which are made the signals; and near it is an encampment.'

In the census of 1891, William Dent was listed as the head of 'Mount Edgcumbe Mansion'. William was the 4th Earl and was, at the time, shown as being widowed and living with his daughter, Lady Edith Hallaran, age 28. Also living at the house were John Duckett, aged 41, who was a Valet and Domestic Servant, and David King, aged 28, who was a Domestic Servant and footman. The census names 17 servants living at the house though many more lived on various parts of the estate. Their jobs included steward room man, housekeeper, cook, ladies maid, house maid, kitchen maid, scullery maid and laundry maid.

The devastation of the Avenue in the Great Blizzard of 1891 is shown here in a picture from the Earl of Mount Edgcumbe collection.

The Handbook for Travellers, published in 1851, states:
'Mount Edgcumbe occupies the western shore of the Sound; and
for the splendour of its prospects, for the charming irregularity of
its surface, for its groves and tasteful gardens, has been long the
boast of the county and a theme for the poet: but language, it is
said, would fail in its description, so the reader must be content
with the observation of the Countess of Ossory, that 'Mount
Edgcumbe has the beauties of all other places added to peculiar
beauties of its own.' By the liberality of the noble owner, the park
is open to the public every Monday; but the stranger, by applying
to Mrs Huss, a bookseller, in Stonehouse, can procure admittance
on other days, but must be then accompanied by a guide. The
house is a castellated building, erected in the reign of Queen Mary,
and commanding a view of the sea through a vista of trees. It
contains several family pictures by Sir Peter Lely and Reynolds,
full-lengths of Charles II, James II, Prince Rupert, and William III,
heads of Charles I and the Duke of Monmouth, and a small
collection by Dutch and Italian masters. But the park and pleasure-
grounds are the principal attraction, and in these the visitor should
direct his attention to the following objects;- The Gardens, three in
number, respectively illustrating the Italian, French, and English
tastes in gardening: the first, with its delightful terrace, orangery,
and Doric conservatory, and its walks converging to a point at a
marble fountain; the second, with its basin and jet d'eau, prim
parterres, and octagon room opening into conservatories; the
third, with its pavilion and noble trees, including the cedar and
cork tree, and exemplifying rather the picturesque and irregular
grouping of nature, than the skill of the gardener. In the vicinity of
these gardens is the Blockhouse, an old fort on the shore of
Barnpool, dating from the reign of Elizabeth; Thomson's Seat; the
Temple of Milton; and the Amphitheatre, a recess in the woods,
The White Seat, near the summit of the park, an alcove
commanding a rare prospect, The Ruin, artificial, but happily
placed, The Cottage, embowered in creeping plants, with a rustic
veranda, The Arch, adjoining a stone seat on the edge of a
precipice overlooking the Sound, The Zig-zag Walks, leading down
the cliffs among rocks and woods, and affording delicious
glimpses of the surrounding scenery, Redding Point, where an
unbounded expanse of ocean bursts upon the sight, Picklecombe,
a sweet secluded dell; and, lastly, the Valley of Hooe Lake, and the
Keeper's Lodge hung with trophies of the chase.'

The trees lining the Avenue. Since 1986, twelve thousand trees have been planted on the Mount Edgcumbe Estate. Unfortunately, the Park was hit by a severe storm in January 1990 which caused devastation to the tree population.

A Victorian etching showing the sweep up to the house. The stucco finish makes the house look quite grand. Before it was bombed in 1941, the house was much larger and contained many irreplaceable treasures belonging to the family.

An etching showing the house from the London News of 1887. The house looks very grand from this angle. The park, at the time, would have been open three times a week to the public and this picture shows some of the visitors.

An early etching showing the house from the Earl's Garden. Amongst the statues in the Earl's Garden are Mercury with a dog - a naked figure draped in a cloak, with a small dog, the head of which is turned towards the god.

An early photo showing the statues featured in the Earl's Garden. The shell seat on the Cedar Lawn is said to contain shells donated by Captain Cook. Other visitors to the house and gardens over the years have included Samuel Pepys, Dr Johnson and the 18th century actor, David Garrick.

A man in a top hat takes it easy reading a book under a tree. At the time, Mount Edgcumbe House, in the background, still had its stucco frontage. A few sheep can be seen grazing in the background.

Mount Edgcumbe has welcomed many famous visitors over the years including Napoleon III (1808 - 1873), who was the Emperor of France and the nephew of Napoleon Bonaparte (1769-1821). After the end of the Franco-German War, Napoleon III stayed at Torquay with his son and visited the estate just three days before the Crown Prince of Prussia (Emperor Frederick 1831-1888) visited with his wife and sons, one of whom was to later become Wilhelm II (1859-1941) more notoriously known as Kaiser Bill who was vilified for causing the First World War. Once again, history is interwoven with connections between the English aristocracy and our German enemies. Of course, the bigger connection here was that Wilhelm II was the grandson of Queen Victoria.

As a guest of Richard Edgcumbe, Willem Van der Velde, the elder,

(1611-1693) painted 'Royal Charles' while at Mount Edgcumbe. The Royal Charles was a ship that was captured by the Dutch in June 1667 during the second Anglo Dutch war of 1665 to 1667. The Royal Charles features in many paintings of the time.

As previously mentioned, Joshua Reynolds (1723-1792) was a regular visitor and was a good friend of the second Lord Edgcumbe, who was a similar age to himself.

Dr Samuel Johnson (1709-1784) visited in 1762, and other guests who visited the estate included General Pasquale di Paoli, who has been described as the Che Guevara of the 18th century. Paoli was introduced to Dr Johnson by James Boswell (1740-1795) who was Johnson's biographer. David Garrick (1717-1779) was another famous visitor. Garrick was an actor and playwright who also managed and produced theatre productions. He was a pupil and friend of Dr Johnson. A Miss Burney also visited Mount Edgcumbe at the time. Her name may not be too well known today but Fanny Burney (1752-1840) was a novelist and diarist and a member of the literary set associated with Dr Johnson. She served as a lady-in-waiting to Queen Charlotte. Burney was admired by Jane Austen, as well as by Dr Johnson and David Garrick. Austen called her, 'England's first woman novelist'. Burney's diaries were published posthumously in 1841 and gave an accurate description of life in the 1700s. The 2nd Baron, Richard (1716-1761) was a close friend of Horace Walpole as was his brother, George, the 1st Earl (1721-1795).George was also friends with Joshua Reynolds, David Garrick and John Opie and became part of the 'Strawberry Hill' set.

Strawberry Hill was the home of Horace Walpole (1717-1797) which he bought in 1748 and which was rebuilt gradually over the years. He was visited by many writers, actors and aristocrats. Walpole was the 4th Earl of Orford and was a politician, a writer, an antiquarian and art historian. He was the son of Sir Robert Walpole and also a cousin of Lord Nelson. After the marriage of Richard, George's son, the second Earl of Edgcumbe (1764-1839) to Sophia Hobart, Fanny Burney wrote, 'he is a most neat little beau and his face has the roses and lillies as finely blended as that of his pretty young wife.'

Richard liked to take part in amateur dramatics and was a musician and he wrote the book, 'Musical Reminiscences of the Earl of Mount Edgcumbe' which contained all the operas he'd heard from 1773 to 1823.

The House in the early 1900s. In 1906, the Earl of Mount Edgcumbe had a staff of 172 including gardeners, house staff, carpenters, stable men and gamekeepers. The Earl was affectionately known as 'Lordy' to his staff.

This photo is from the Earl of Mount Edcumbe Collection and features Mount Edgcumbe's Fire Brigade in 1910. The cart contains small wooden ladders A hose can be seen attached at the back end of the cart. The stables behind were built in 1850 and contained a dairy, a smithy and a sawmill.

Here we see Mr Chamberlain, the carter, in this photo from the Earl of Mount Edcumbe Collection. The shire horse is laden with horse brasses. Horse brasses were highly prized by carters and in the late 1800s, prize or merit awards were given during horse parades.

This photo from the Earl of Mount Edgcumbe collection shows a shooting party. A dog waits on the left ready to retrieve any bagged animals.

A Guide to the Coasts of Devon and Cornwall, published in 1859, mentions:

'One night, when Sir Richard kept revel and dance in the old hall, a body of armed maskers from Plymouth appeared coming up the avenues. At once, the doughty old knight called in his servants to resist with sword and buckler; but the lighted torches revealed only armour of paper and helmets of tin, and he merrily invited them to take part in the measure. On retiring, their chief courteously bowed, thanked the knight for his good cheer, and assured him that of an enemy he was converted into his chief friend, commending at the same time to his notice a nephew, heir to his broad lands, who was there disguised as a nymph. Months passed away, and the young man was married before the altar at Maker to Sir Richard's fair daughter. It was a fitting place for a lover's tryst, with its lawns of soft velvet turf, its pines and chestnuts, broad groves of cedar, oak, and beech; on the upland, arbutus, laurustinus, Portugal laurel, and dark-leaved myrtle; pleasant shades and recesses for repose, opening inward from sunny glades; wild paths along the brink of dark ravines; beauty mingled with the grandeur of majestic heights; and over all the freshness of the sea and air, as the flowing waves climbed the black reefs of rock below. In 1779, the Earl of Mount Edgcumbe cut down all his fine trees, as an alarm of a French invasion very generally prevailed. The grounds still are very attractive, but disfigured by silly artificial ruins. The Orangery was designed by Lord Camelford. The ivied remains of the old Blockhouse at Barnpool, by the waterside, are of the time of Elizabeth. Below it is the saluting battery, restored in 1747, and in 1800 mounted with 21 French cannon. King George III visited the house on the 21st August, 1789. Garrick wrote an epigram upon it, beginning -
'This mount all the mounts of Great Britain surpasses,
Tis the haunt of the muses - this mount of Parnassus.'

A passage within the pages of The Ports, Harbours, Watering-places and Coast Scenery of Great Britain, published 1842, stated:
The house at Mount Edgcumbe was erected about the year 1550, in the castellated style, with circular towers at the corners. About seventy years ago (1772) those towers were pulled down, and rebuilt in their present octangular form.

This photo from the Earl of Mount Edgcumbe collection shows Kenelm, the 6th Earl, amongst the bombed ruins of Mount Edgcumbe House. It's hard to imaging from this photo that the house would ever be restored.

This photo from the Earl of Mount Edgcumbe collection is taken from the Earl's Garden and shows the blackened roof tops of the house. The rafters of part of the roof can still be seen.

This photo from the Earl of Mount Edgcumbe collection shows the house after it was gutted by German bombs on Tuesday 22nd April 1941. Unfortunately, because of the bombing, many of the Edgcumbe family's possessions were destroyed. These included rare furniture and paintings. Three generations of the Edgcumbe family were painted by Joshua Reynolds and all but one were destroyed.

It was said that both Adolf Hitler and Herman Goering fancied Mount Edgcumbe House as their country retreat were they to win the war so neither would have been best pleased when it was bombed.

In 1944, concrete roads were laid in preparation for the D-Day invasion. After being bombed, the house was left as a shell until 1958. Adrian Gilbert Scott was commissioned to rebuild the house using concrete floors and a steel frame. After the Second World War, the house had the rendering removed from its walls leaving its present red sandstone appearance. The entrance at the North front still has its original 16th century doorway and is surrounded by late 17th century Doric pilasters and a pediment. The house is decorated in neo-Georgian style.

An internal shot of the bombed house is seen in this photo from the Earl of Mount Edgcumbe Collection. During the War, the railings from the house were taken away to help as part of the war effort. Railings were collected from all over the country to be melted down and used in munitions. Although this practice united communities in their search for scrap metal, none of it was ever used. Unfortunately, although the exercise was said to boost morale, many of the railings collected around the country were simply dumped.

Two photos of the house as it is today. The red-bricked house is smaller than it once was and has lost its stucco finish. It is still an impressive building however and, looking at it today, it's hard to imagine that it was renovated in just 1964. Sections of the walls are older than 450 years.

Three

The Obelisk

There is a story that the Obelisk was erected to celebrate the life of the Countess of Mount Edgcumbe's pet pig, Cupid. However, other sources say that the Obelisk was erected, in its current position, by Timothy Brett in 1770 in honour of his friend, George, the 3rd Baron of Edgcumbe. Brett was a former Commissioner of the Navy.
The Obelisk was originally sited where the Folly now stands. The 50 ft monument has been used as a navigational point by various shipping in the Sound over the years.

Cupid the pig was said to have been buried in a gold casket beneath the obelisk when he died in 1768. In the book, 'Animals Graves and Memorials' by Jan Toms (Shire Publications 2006), it says that when the obelisk was moved to its present position, in 1770, nothing was found. However, the date of 1770 may be misleading as the obelisk appears in its present position on shipping maps as early as 1768. As this was the year that Cupid died, it might be reasonable to assume that he is buried beneath the obelisk in its present position.
It is known that Fern Dell once contained an urn that commemorated Cupid but this has since disappeared. However, it is also recorded that

Cupid was buried at Fern Dell and this was noted by George III and Queen Charlotte.

The dates prove confusing. For instance, the Folly was said to be erected on the spot where the Obelisk originally stood. However, the folly was erected in 1747 so how could Cupid have died and been buried beneath the obelisk, in its original position, in 1768? Research shows that the obelisk in its original position had already collapsed when the work to build the folly got underway.

Cupid led a charmed life eating at the dinner table of the Edgcumbes and even accompanying the Countess, Emma Gilbert, on trips to London. The Edgcumbes love of their pets can be seen at Fern Dell where many of them are buried. When a later Countess of Mount Edgcumbe, Caroline Georgia, died in 1909, she requested that a fountain be erected near the shore at Cremyll which bore the inscription, 'For the Doggies'.

In ' A Complete Parochial History of the County', published in 1870, it states, **'In the Cypress Grove is a monument to the memory of Timothy Brett Esq, one of the commissioners of the Navy, who, about the year 1770 erected the obelisk on the knoll near Cremyll as a memorial for his regard of his friend, George, the 3rd Baron of Edgcumbe.'**

At the time, George was still alive and serving in the Royal Navy. During 1770, he was promoted to Vice Admiral and was appointed Vice Treasurer of Ireland.

Today, the obelisk is almost hidden away on a hill behind the Mount Edgcumbe Arms. There is no plaque on the monument to say who it is dedicated to and it's probably seen better days. It's hard to imagine now that it once stood where the folly stands.

To add to the confusion, the date, '1st July,1867', has been carved into the base of the obelisk. Beside the date is the name, 'R F Crowther'. This mystery has, however, since been solved. Richard Crowther was in training during the 1860s on the boy's training ship, 'HMS Impregnable' which was moored off Cremyll. One day, Richard wandered towards the obelisk from the training ship armed with a hammer and chisel and left the inscription and date. He was born in 1853 so would have been 14 years old in 1867 when he left his mark. Cupid's remains may or may not be buried beneath the Obelisk but please don't go looking for them!

Four

The Barrow

The Barrow is a Bronze Age burial mound which dates from around 1200 BC. It was used as a prospect mound during the 18th century and was also used as a viewing point to enjoy the surrounding gardens, the park and the City of Plymouth. It has also at one time been used as a firing range and a military camp was situated close by.

There are many other Bronze Age settlements in the area. Bronze Age barrows can be found near to the cliff edge at Tregonhawke, Rame Head, and Wiggle Cliff near Whitsand Bay.

During the 1800s, it became a popular pastime for the wealthy and well educated to carry out the task of barrow digging. Although this pastime revealed many aspects of the land's history, untold damage was also done at the same time.

Flint tools discovered in the Rame Head area suggest that people inhabited the region as long ago as the Mesolithic period. There is evidence of Bronze Age barrows all over Cornwall.

Barrows or Tumuli, as they are sometimes known, consist of a mound of earth and stone placed over a grave. They can be found throughout the world. Tumulus is the Latin word for 'mound' or 'small hill'. There are many types of barrows and as well as the remains of the deceased, they can also contain pottery vessels and weapons and tools.

During the Bronze Age, the remains of the deceased were quite often cremated and placed in vessels which would then be set into the ground beneath the burial mound. Mounds were placed in areas of importance.

There seems to be no record of the barrow at Mount Edgcumbe being excavated though it is quite possible that, at one time, this has taken place.

The Bronze-age horns which are kept in Mount Edgcumbe House are not from a local source but come from Ireland.

Five

The Orangery and the Italian Garden

The Orangery was built in 1760. It was built to house orange trees from Constantinople. Unfortunately, when it was bombed in 1941, many of the trees, some of which were over 100 years old, were destroyed. It was restored in 1953.

In later years, the Orangery has been used as a cafe and restaurant. The Italian Garden was laid out between 1750 and 1809. Its main features are the mermaid fountain, the statues of Apollo, Venus and Bacchus, the bust of Ludovico Ariosto, the neatly trimmed lawns and the fine array of orange trees.

The Italian Garden in all its splendour.

In the pages of 'Passages from the Diaries of Mrs. Philip Lybbe Powys of Hardwick House, Oxon: A.D. 1756-1808, published in 1899, she mentions, **'In the orangery are some of the largest fruit I have ever seen...'**
Pall Mall Magazine, published in 1897, mentions the Orangery within its pages:
'In the Winter, they find refuge in the Orangery, a fine building erected in the last century from the designs of Lord Camelford of Bocconnoc. The handsome marble fountain in the middle of the garden was a present from Lord Bessborough to Richard, second Earl, to whom, as well as his daughter Emma, he had stood godfather.'

Extracts from The West Briton Newspaper in the Quarter Century from 1810 to 1835 mention:
'Fete Champetre at Mount Edgcumbe
On the 14th instant, the Earl of Mount Edgcumbe and Lady Emma gave a breakfast to a select party in the flower garden at his estate in the Orangery, a noble building of the Doric order, one hundred feet in length.'

The Story of my Life : Marie Queen of Roumania, published in 1934, mentions visits to the gardens:
'Beyond Devonport Harbour lay Mount Edgcumbe, a marvellously beautiful country seat belonging to a courteous lord of the same name. He had opened wide his gates to us, and Mount Edgcumbe became our dearest playing-ground, to which we went nearly every day. Suspended above the sea, it had lovely drives through beautiful woods and over undulating downs, a noble estate which became as familiar to us as though it had been our home.
In parts, the vegetation was almost that of the Riviera and you could drive through whole avenues of evergreens, and there was also a laurel walk with a marvellous view over the sea. But our favourite haunt was the Italian Garden. Planted on the water's edge, it was easily reached by boat from our side of the harbour; a shady retreat full of poetry, it had terraces, colonnades, flagged walks and secret-looking pools. It also had the classical Orangery. Flanked by beautiful woods, it was there that I picked my last English primroses and I have an enchanted remembrance of how they grew in pale, fragrant clumps all over the banks and up in amongst the century-old trees.'

The mermaid fountain features in a Nicholas Condy painting of the Italian Garden dated 1816. The fountain was a gift which was given to Richard, the second Earl, by Lord Bessborough in 1809. Many of the statues displayed in the garden would have been gathered during Grand Tours of Europe and neighbouring countries. Richard, the second Baron Edgcumbe (1716-1761) had his Grand Tour extended as a young man to curb his gambling habits. When he returned in 1744, after a seven year stay in Turkey, he brought with him orange trees and a collection of classical antiquities.

Richard had a relatively short life, dying in his middle forties, and he only held the title for three years. He enjoyed drawing and poetry and was a close friend of Horace Walpole who was the 4th Earl of Orford.

The statues of Venus, Apollo and Bacchus. All date from around 1785. Bacchus, or Dionysus, is the god of wine and ecstatic liberation. He was the youngest of the great Greek gods.

The statues would have been collected during the time of George the 1st Earl of Mount Edgcumbe (1721-1795). He had a great interest in antiquities like his brother, Richard, the 2nd Baron. The statues would have been collected in the later part of his life when George was in his sixties. As a young man, George served in the Royal Navy rapidly rising in the ranks from midshipman to Rear Admiral in 1772.

Richard (1764-1839), the 2nd Earl and the son of George, spent time in Italy during his Grand Tour and he married Sophia Hobart in 1789. She died at the young age of 38 but they had five children who shared a love of gardens and trees. The Italian Garden, the French Garden and much of the plantations and drives were laid out during this time.

The statue of Apollo. Apollo was the Greek god of prophecy, music, healing, poetry and fine arts. Perhaps he is more recognised as god of light and the sun. He was worshipped by the Greeks and later, the Romans.

Interestingly, when the statue of Apollo, in the Italian Garden, was repaired in the 1990s, a Marigold glove was used as a mould to make a new hand.

Views of the Orangery and the Italian Garden. In the top picture can be seen the statues of Venus, Apollo and Bacchus as well as the Mermaid Fountain and several orange trees. The bottom picture shows the gardens and the Orangery in the background.

The statue of Venus on the balustrades above the Italian Garden.
Venus was a Roman goddess associated with love, beauty and fertility.

More Famous Homes of Great Britain and their stories by Alfred Henry
Malan, published in 1902, said:
'The Italian Garden is celebrated for its numerous and splendid
orange trees, said to be - and probably with truth- the finest in
England, and even superior to those in the gardens of Tuileries. Be
this as it may, they are certainly magnificent specimens and some
of the trees must be more than a hundred and fifty years old,
having been brought from Constantinople by Richard, second
Lord Edgcumbe, when, as a very young man, he was sent on his
travels to keep him out of mischief. They are remarkably
healthy, and, in due season, are white with blossom or golden with
fruit. In the winter, they find refuge in the Orangery a fine building
erected in the last century from the designs of Lord Camelford.'

At the end of the Italian Gardens is the bust of Ludovico Ariosto (1474-1535) who was a sixteenth century Italian poet and the author of 'Orlando Furioso' (1532). The bust dates from 1785 and is one of the souvenirs from the family's Grand Tours of Europe which were used to enhance the courtyard. There are two tablets of white marble nearby. The first, underneath in Italian text, reads:

'Vicino al lido donde a poco a poco
Si salendo in verso il colle ameno
Mirti e cedri e naranci, e lauri il loco
E mille altri souvi arbori han perio
Serpillo dall odorifero terreno
Tanta scarila, che'n mar sentive
La fa ogni vento, che, da terra sfare.'

This translates as:

'Near to the shore, from whence with soft ascent
Rises the pleasant hill, there is a place.
With many an orange, cedar, myrtle, bay,
And every shrub of grateful scent adorn'd.
The rose, the lily, crocus, serpolet.
Such sweets diffuse the odoriferous ground,
That from the land each gently breathing gale
Wafts forth the balmy fragrance to the sea.'

Six

The Garden Battery

The Garden Battery was originally a saluting point with 21 guns in place to greet visitors. It was restored in 1747 but was rebuilt between 1862 and 1863 as part of Plymouth's sea defences.

An early group on a picnic shown relaxing in front of the battery. The canons can be seen on top of the battery and in the background is the Royal William Yard.

The Devonshire and Cornwall illustrated, published in 1832, mentions the earlier Battery:
'The battery in front, after long neglect, was restored in 1747 and in 1800 was remounted with twenty-one French eight-pounders, all purchased from prizes. The views from this spot comprehend the whole of Barnpool, St. Nicholas Island, Plymouth, the Breakwater and Sound, Mount Batten, Staddon Heights, the Mewstone, together with several striking portions of the home scenery.'

The United Service Magazine, published in 1867, said:

'Mount Edgcumbe battery, seven guns, constructed of granite like the rest, and prepared to receive iron shields; all of these are nearly completed, those at Eastern King and Western King (earthworks) are completed, and they command the channel for light-draught vessels between Mount Edgcumbe and Drake's Island.'

The Earl's Battery was positioned on top of the Garden Battery in 1847. The Garden Battery was still in use in 1911 when it was armed with two quick-firing guns. Quick-firing was introduced in the late 1890s and this allowed the artillery pieces to fire shells much more rapidly than older weapons. They were originally introduced on Naval vessels and had a marked effect during battles.

During the Second World War, the battery was armed to defend the river during enemy attacks.

Etched in the stone is the date, 1862, and the initials of Victoria, 'V R'.

In A Journal of a Tour around the Southern coasts of England by John Henry Manners, published in 1805, it said:

'A little way from the alcove, we passed a battery of 21 guns, which are fired as way of salute on the King's birthday etc.'

A single canon protrudes over the battery wall. There are still three canons mounted on the battery. These were captured from the French and are marked, 'R F' (Republic Francaise) with a Cap of Liberty and the date.

A view looking back towards the Blockhouse over the balustrades edging the Garden Battery.

This part of the battery is known as Queen Victoria's landing stage and it was commissioned by William Henry, the 4th Earl of Edgcumbe (1832-1917). The cast iron wrought work has the date, 1862' shown along with Victoria's monogram, 'V R'. In the background can be seen Devil's Point and the Royal William Yard.

Seven

The English Garden

The English Garden House was built in 1729 and was extended in 1820. The garden was laid out in 1770 and it contains irregular lawns and also features many rare trees including a Magnolia, several Cork Oak, a Ginko, a Fox-glove tree, an Indian Bean tree, a Japanese Red Cedar, a Wych Hazel and a Mimosa.

If you've ever wondered what once lay inside the building in the English Gardens then the Devonshire and Cornwall Illustrated, published in 1832, reveals the answer:

'Within the English garden, which is of much greater extent than either of those previously described, are many majestic and beautiful trees, including several magnolias, Libernian and Virginian cedars and some large cork trees. Here, likewise, is a neat pavilion of the Doric order, containing a bath, the marble basin of which is supplied with hot and cold water from the mouths of two bronze dolphins.'

Richard, the 1st Baron of Edgcumbe with his beloved dog, painted by Sir Joshua Reynolds.

After the death of his dog, Richard, the 1st Baron of Edgcumbe, had its skeleton mounted and displayed in a case within the English Garden House. He would often visit and talk to his deceased friend. When the dog's body was removed in the 1800s, and probably buried at Fern Dell, there were reports of ghostly scratching as if the dog was trying to get back into the Garden House.

The Garden House in 1729 would have formed part of the then wilderness garden. When the new garden was laid out in the 1770s, the house was used as a focal point. It has been used by the family for picnics and for listening to music. In 1820, it was extended to contain a room with a sunken bath and two new wings.

Many have pointed out that although it is called the English Garden, it contains many shrubs that are not native to England.

A letter of Harriet, Countess of Granville, written in 1815 to Lady G Morpeth, reads:

'The English Garden is like the plantation at Tixal, with magnolias and arbutus, large trees and benches and comforts in abundance. There is a great bath, a room with tables and a divan around it.'

The Plymouth and Devonport Guide by Henry Edmund Carrington, published in 1828, read:
'The English Garden is more simply arranged than either of the others. It is of considerable extent and is laid out in beds of shrubs and flowers, traversed by gravel walks, which are so managed as to conceal the real limits of the enclosure. It contains many beautiful and majestic trees, among which are several fine magnolias, cedars of Lebanus and Virginia, and a few large cork-trees. This delightful retreat is decorated with a square Doric pavilion, containing a sitting and dressing- room, and a bath, supplied with hot and cold water from the mouths of two bronze dolphins. A bench in the garden is inscribed with the following lines from Cowper.
Prospects however lovely may be seen
Till half their beauties fade; the weary sight,
Too well acquainted with their smiles, slides off
Fastidious, seeking less familiar scenes.
Then snug enclosures in the sheltered vale, Where frequent hedges intercept the eye, Delight us, happy to renounce a while, Not senseless of its charms, what still we love, That such short absence may endear it more.'

A cork oak tree within the English Garden.

Close to the English Garden is the Rose Garden which dates from the late 1700s. New gardens include the American Garden, laid out in 1989, the New Zealand Garden, also laid out in 1989 and complete with geyser, and the Jubilee Garden which was completed in 2002.

The French Garden

The French Garden was laid out in1803. It was surrounded by bay hedges with yew and oak trees. A statue of Mercury once stood at the far end of the garden and this was reflected in the convex mirror hanging in the Octagon room. On either side of the room is a conservatory.

The Devonshire and Cornwall illustrated, published in 1832, mentions the French Gardens:

'In the French garden is an elegant octagonal room, opening into Conservatories : at the back of this apartment, a pleasing illusion is created by the removal of a picture; a small antique statue of Meleager is then discovered, behind which is a mirror, that reflects most of the various objects within the garden. In this division, opposite to a very beautiful magnolia tree, is a votive urn and tablet, inscribed in memory of Sophia, late Countess of Mount

Edgcumbe, who died in 1806, and to whose genius these grounds owe many of their improvements. The inscription, from its elegant simplicity, merits to be recorded ; it is as follows :
To the memory of her
Whose taste embellished,
Whose presence added charms,
To these retreats,
Herself the brightest ornament,
This urn is erected,
In the spot she loved.'

A couple enjoy the peace in the French Garden in this photo from the Earl of Mount Edgcumbe collection. The French Garden was a favourite retreat for Sophia, Countess of Mount Edgcumbe who died in 1806.

The shell fountain in the middle of the French Garden. Coins are regularly thrown into the pond by visitors to the estate.

The Timothy Brett memorial is supported by three tortoises.

Travels through North America, during the years 1825 and 1826 by His Highness Bernhard, Duke of Saxe-Weimar Eisenach, published in 1828, says of Sophia, Lady Edgcumbe:

'We saw the monument of Lady Mount Edgcumbe, who died in 1806, to whom the park is indebted for most of its improvements. It is told of her that she was twice buried; the first time she remained three days in a vault, lying in her coffin, and was aroused by a thief cutting off her finger to steal a ring: she left the grave, took refuge in a neighbouring house, made herself known, and was re-conveyed to her castle, where she subsequently lived several years and gave birth to children.'

The story about Lady Edgcumbe being revived by a thief is an interesting one. This seems to be an accurate tale that has been repeated many times as in The Gentleman's Magazine of 1853:

'Another circumstance, far more extraordinary than any yet related in connection with Cotehele, is so well authenticated that not even a doubt rests about its truth, and with the relation of it this paper shall be brought to a close. It refers to the mother of Sir Richard Edgcumbe, knight, who, in 1748, was created Baron of Mount Edgcumbe.

The family were residing at Cotehele (I do not know the date or the year) when Lady Edgcumbe became much indisposed, and, to all appearance, died. How long after is not stated, but her body was deposited in the family vault of the parish church. The interment had not long taken place before the sexton (who must have heard from the nurse or the servants that she was buried with something of value upon her) went down into the vault at midnight, and contrived to force open the coffin. A gold ring was on her ladyship's finger, which, in a hurried way, he attempted to draw off, but not readily succeeding, he pressed with great violence the finger. Upon this the body moved in the coffin, and such was the terror of the man that he ran away as fast as he could, leaving his lantern behind him. Lady Edgcumbe arose, astonished at finding herself dressed in grave-clothes, and numbered with the tenants of the vault. She took up the lantern, and proceeded at once to the mansion of Cotehele. The terror, followed by the rejoicing of her family and household, which such a resurrection from the tomb occasioned may well be conceived. Exactly five years after this circumstance she became the mother of Sir Richard Edgcumbe who was created baron.'

However, the mother of Sir Richard Edgcumbe was Lady Ann Montagu and not Sophia. Later versions of the story tell of the same events befalling Emma (1791-1872), the daughter of Richard, the 2nd Earl (1764-1839) and Lady Sophia Hobart (1768-1806) and this version has appeared in many books. Although the tale seems like it might be true, the exact details seem to have been muddled over the years.

The memorial dedicated to Timothy Brett was built in 1791. The memorial was commissioned by George, the 1st Earl of Edgcumbe who was a close Naval friend of Brett. The monument from the Coade factory features a stock design which appears in other places, though the design is attributed to James Wyatt. One of the three sides shows a medallion which bears a Latin inscription. This translates to, 'Monument sacred to the bravest man and greatest friend Timothy Brett 1791'.

Nine

Fern Dell

Fern Dell, also known as the Pets Cemetery, contains the graves of many of the Edgcumbe's dogs including Banjo who died in 1895, Louie who died in 1949 and Pepper who died in 1920. It is felt to be a gloomy place being set down from the other gardens in an old quarry pit and because of its many tall ferns and over growing ivy.

Perhaps the cemetery was also once the resting place of Cupid, the pig belonging to the Countess of Mount Edgcumbe. The pig accompanied her everywhere, much to the amusement of her friends. When it died, a Kingsbridge man wrote an ode to it which read:

'Ode to the Countess of Mount Edgcumbe on the death of her pet pig Cupid:
Oh dry those tears so round and big,
Nor waste in sight your precious wind,
Death only takes a little pig
Your Lord and Son are still behind.'

In The Works with Acopious Index, published in 1823, it refers to the grave of Cupid:

'This pig, Cupid, who many years ago fell in love with the Earl, has a monument erected to his memory, with an inscription on it by Lord Valletort, the Earl's son.'

A select collection of poems with notes by J. Nichols, published in 1780, mentions the beloved pig:

'A Gentleman from the neighbourhood of Mount Edgcumbe, telling Mr Nicholls that Cupid died a mere brute, occasioned him to write this Epitaph:

Here in the dirt doth Cupid lie
Cupid the pig, of swine of pride
Mov'd to a palace from a sty
He ate and drank, he liv'd and died
Let such as have no higher view
Consider, for tis past a jest
How many a man (as wise as Cu)
Lives like a lord, dies like a beast.'

From the passage from The Works with Acopious Index, it would appear that Cupid was buried somewhere where his grave was marked with a plaque. Perhaps, he is still there. However, Fern Dell was laid out between 1789 and 1820 and the earlier date is some 21 years after Cupid died. The was an urn dedicated to Cupid at Fern Dell but unfortunately, this monument has now been removed. On one of his visits to Mount Edgcumbe, George III, on reportedly seeing Cupid's headstone, remarked to Queen Charlotte, 'It's the family vault, Charley! The family vault!'

The area has been replanted with ivies and tree ferns in recent years and the seats and headstones have been repaired.

Although a somewhat eerie and quiet place, it's interesting to visit and imagine the lives the pets had with their owners and the many well known people of the day that visited the estate.

The fountain features a face which seems suitable to the cold and eerie setting. Water, at one time, seems to have spouted from its mouth into the drinking trough below.

The Devonshire and Cornwall illustrated, published in 1832, mentions Fern Dell:
'The walk leading from the English garden towards the Blockhouse, descends into a deep excavation, or quarry, which, from being embosomed amidst lofty evergreens, overspread with parasitical plants, and scattered about with antique urns, sarcophagi, and other funereal vestiges, assumes the character of an ancient Cemetery - at one extremity, to increase the interest from association, amidst a heap of architectural fragments, lies a fine capital of the Corinthian order, brought from the ruins of Alexandria.'

The fountain, with a drinking trough, in a corner of Fern Dell.

Several of the graves near to the seating area.

The grave of Banjo. The inscription reads, 'In memory of Banjo. Son of Bang of Saltram. For 10 years my faithful companion. Died November 18th 1895. C.E.E.'

A close up of the eerie face featured on the water fountain.

Ten

The Great Hedge

The great hedge is made up of Ilex and measures 10 metres high. It forms a giant windbreak that protects the gardens from the cold easterly winds.
The hedge would have been the first thing many travellers saw when landing at Barn Pool.

A photo from the Earl of Mount Edgcumbe Collection showing the gardeners, Mr Walters and Mr Phillips, trimming the hedge. The Earl is in the centre of the picture which also shows a small dog.
Long wooden ladders and hand shears were used at the time by the two men to slowly trim the hedge.
Nash's Pall Mall Magazine, published in 1897,said:
'One is transported to Italy. No cold blasts touch this favoured spot, which for nearly a mile is planted with evergreen trees and shrubs from the crown of the hill to the verge of the cliff. Here the road winds past walls of laurel, laurestinus and arbatus, the sea sparkles through the pine branches and the sunlight gleams on polished camellia.'

Shown here is the great hedge with the Blockhouse on the right of the picture. The grassed area on the right leading towards the Blockhouse was once a bowling green which was laid in around 1670.

The entrance in the hedge which leads to the formal gardens.

In the pages of Lord Byron and some of his Contemporaries by Leigh Hunt, published in 1828, the author visits Mount Edgcumbe and various estates in Cornwall. He mentions:

'In the grounds is a bowling green, the scene of a once fashionable movement amusement, now grown out of use; which is a pity. Fashion cannot too much identify itself with what is healthy; nor has England been 'Merry England,' since late hours and pallid faces came into vogue.'

It seems that bowling was a very popular pastime in the times of Drake and after in the 1600s but died out in later years. King Henry VIII enjoyed lawn bowling but banned the lower classes from playing because he feared it would stop bowyers, fletchers, stringers and arrowhead makers from carrying on their trade. He levied a fee of £100 for anyone who wanted to keep a green but also stated that it only be used for private purposes and he forbid anyone to **'play at any bowle or bowles in open space out of his own garden or orchard'**.

By the time the green at Mount Edgcumbe was laid out in the 1670s, the Monarch had changed several times but it was still seen a pastime for the upper-classes and the ban, amazingly, continued until 1845.

Eleven

The Blockhouse

The Blockhouse is a Tudor fort that saw action during the Civil War. It was built in 1545 to defend the mouth of the Tamar and also to protect Stonehouse which lay opposite.

During the Civil War, Colonel Piers Edgcumbe (1610-1667) sided with the Royalists but, with the Parliamentarians occupying Plymouth, he wisely moved to Cotehele. Mount Edgcumbe was attacked several times by the Parliamentarian forces. A Lieutenant Colonel Martin attacked Mount Edgcumbe and captured three guns from the blockhouse before attacking Maker Church, which had been fortified by the Royalist garrison of Mount Edgcumbe. At the same time, Martin also captured the fort at Cawsand. In May 1644, Mount Edgcumbe was again attacked, this time by Captain Haynes. Outbuildings were set on fire and the Banqueting Hall was damaged. The Royalists of Edgcumbe refused to surrender but in the following year, Piers Edgcumbe surrendered to Sir Thomas Fairfax under the condition that he kept his family estate intact.

The Devonshire and Cornwall Illustrated, published in 1832, mentions the Blockhouse:

'On the margin of Barn-pool, is the Blockhouse, now partly in ruins, and picturesquely overgrown with ivy. This, with a similar fort at Devil's Point, the opposite promontory, was erected for the defence of the Harbour, in the reign of Queen Elizabeth, and is thus noticed in Carew's Survey of Cornwall.'

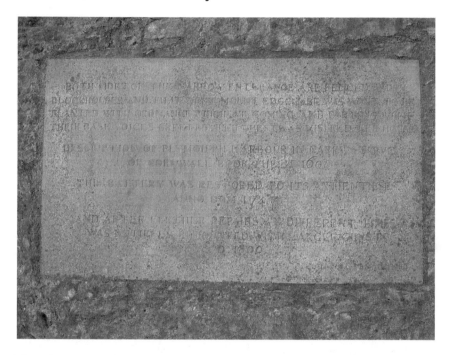

The above tablet set in the wall of the Blockhouse features text taken from Carew's survey of 1620 and reads:

'Both sides of the narrow entrance are fenced with Blockhouses and that near to Mount Edgcumbe was to be planted in ordinance, which, at coming and departing with their base voices greeting such guests as visited the house.'

The Blockhouse became less used as a defence when the Battery was built on the shore in 1747 and then enlarged between 1862 and 1863. There is another Blockhouse still standing to this day which can be seen of the rocks opposite.

The view looking out through the door of the Blockhouse. It used to be possible to get onto the roof of the Blockhouse which gave splendid views out to the Sound but the stairway upwards has been boarded off for many years, probably because it was felt that it was too dangerous for people to climb and sit on the top.

Twelve

Thomson's Seat

Thomson's seat is named after the poet, James Thomson. It was built in the 1760's and a quotation from Thomson's poem, 'The Seasons', appears on the wall inside. It reads:

'On either hand like a long wintry forest,
Groves of masts shot up their spires,
The bellying sheets between possessed the breezy void.'

James Thomson (1700-1748) was a Scottish poet and playwright. Famous for 'The Seasons', he also wrote the words to 'Rule Britannia'.

From the seat inside the Doric pavilion can be seen views of the Sound and Cremyll as well as much of Plymouth.

Behind Thomson's seat are the remains of several old greenhouses which date to a time before 1844.

Thomson seems to have been forgotten by many and the building is quite often, and wrongly, referred to as 'Thompson's Seat'.

The tree to the right of Thomson's Seat, a Wellingtonia Sequoiadendron Giganteum, was planted in 1853 from a seed brought from California. The tree was named after the Duke of Wellington who had died the previous year.

Thirteen

Barn Pool

Barn Pool is a sheltered deep water area of Mount Edgcumbe. A large polished stone axe was found by divers near a reef at Barn Pool .The area is likely to have been above sea-level during Neolithic times. The area was also used by the Vikings in 997. There is a shipwreck further offshore, the Catharina von Flensburg, which sank there in 1786.

This photo shows a mock battle put on to entertain the Royal visitors to Barn Pool in 1880. Ships that took part in the battle included the training brigs, 'Liberty Pilot' and 'Nautilus'.

Famous visitors who would have landed at Barn Pool include George III, Queen Charlotte and Princess Amelia who visited on the 25th August 1789.

A Londoner's Walk to the Land's End and a trip to the Scilly Isles by Walter White, published in 1879, says:

'George III and Queen Charlotte, with three of the princesses, took breakfast, when they were the guests of the Earl of Mount Edgcumbe.'

And an account in Lake's Parochial History of the County of Cornwall confirms:

'On Tuesday, August 25th, 1789, his Majesty King George the Third honoured this old mansion with his presence, and sate in this chair, while he condescended to take a breakfast with the Earl and Countess of Mount Edgcumbe.
Their Royal Highnesses the Princess Royal, Princess Augusta and Princess Elizabeth also honoured them at the same time with their presence.'

The Plymouth and Devonport Guide : With Sketches of the Surrounding Scenery by Henry Edmund Carrington, published in 1828, describes Barn Pool:

'And what a delicious spot is Barnpool in the sunset hour! Its piled-up woods are hushed in the deepest tranquillity, and, indeed, the whole scene reposes in as intense a stillness as the lonely isles which have here now been discovered in far-off seas by those who go down to the great deep in ships - isles where the flowers have withered unpicked on their stems, and the fruits have decayed untouched on the bough through countless ages. The dark recesses of the woods - the little temple dedicated to Milton - the irregular lawns, dotted with little oases of tangled shrubs in which the hare loves to nestle.'

Charles Darwin's journey is mentioned in the Quarterly Review of 1840:

'On the 27th November, 1831, the well-manned, well-appointed and well-provided Beagle sailed from Barn Pool, and having circumnavigated the globe, and accomplished all the objects the expedition had in view, as far was practical, she anchored at Falmouth on the 2nd October, 1836, after and absence of four years and nine months.'

Darwin had lived in Plymouth for two months before his famous voyage around the world in HMS Beagle. The ship was captained by Robert Fitzroy. Darwin, who was then just 22 years old, joined the crew as a naturalist. He had a wealthy family who paid the £30 fare needed to travel on the Beagle.

Before leaving, he visited and walked the Mount Edgcumbe estate, and on various occasions visited Rame Head, Millbrook, Whitsand Bay and Cawsand, which he wrote in his journal of the 17th December, 1831, was **'one of the most curiously built places I ever saw. It is situated in a very pretty little bay, which shelters numerous fishing and smuggling boats from the sea.'**

Barn Pool is also famous for being the area where American servicemen left for the D-Day invasion during 1944. The troops were stationed at Maker Camp. The deep anchorage by Barn Pool made it the ideal access point for military vehicles. A slipway was laid which consisted of a material known as chocolate box hards. Parts of these can still be seen today on the shoreline.

In June 1944, thousands of American troops left from here for the shores of Northern France.

Every year, Mount Edgcumbe hosts an event showing off vintage military vehicles and equipment. The gathering takes place on the land around Barn Pool.

The view down to Barn Pool towards the point where the Americans left for D-Day.

If you walk from Empacombe towards the Obelisk, you will find several old disused buildings on your right. These were used by the US army as a fuel depot. On the shore, near to the depot, can still be seen the area where the pipes ran towards the water's edge where the River Tamar would have been full with American ships preparing for the D-Day attacks on Utah Beach in Normandy. The pipes have been removed from the shore but still lie in a pile nearby over 60 years later. The buildings are mainly empty and some have graffiti on them. The buildings original use during the war is probably long forgotten by many people.

During the Second World War much of the Mount Edgcumbe Estate was occupied by the War Department. This included the park land adjoining Maker Church, the Garden Battery, Beechwood Cottages, the roads and drives and Barrow Park. The Admiralty requisitioned Barn Pool and the Amphitheatre, the Maker Fuel Depots, Obelisk Field, Cremyll, the tennis courts and electricity plant, the sheep park and the stables. A pipeline was installed at Lower Chapel Fields to fuel the ships heading for D-Day in 1944. This remained the property of the Admiralty until 1954. A report was made concerning the damage to the formal gardens between 1943 and 1947.

Some of the trees within the park still carry the names of the US servicemen who left from Barn Pool. These ones read, above, **'McCalip, 1944, Schott'** and, below, **'J W 1944'** and **'Earl R Lawton June, 1944.'**

Two winter views showing the road sweeping down to Barn Pool. It's hard to imagine, in such a tranquil scene, the events of 1945.

Barn Pool looking towards Milton's Temple. The waters here have welcomed many ships and their visitors for several hundred years, including royalty and the celebrities of the day.

Remains of the chocolate box hards laid by the American servicemen in 1944. These can still be found scattered all over the beach.

Fourteen

Milton's Temple

Milton's Temple was built in 1755 and is of a circular Ionic style. John Milton died in 1674 long before the temple was built but his words from Paradise Lost seem to aptly describe Mount Edgcumbe.

A view looking from the temple up into the park.

A letter of Harriet, Countess of Granville, written in 1815 to Lady G Morpeth, reads:
'In another part of the place, there is a temple with a bust of Milton and lines descriptive of the place from Paradise Lost. Lord Mount Edgcumbe is not a good Adam, but he was very civil and gave us a great deal of fruit but very little of his company.'
The bust of Milton seems to have disappeared from the temple over the years. John Milton was born in 1608 and during his lifetime was a poet, author and civil servant. During the Civil War, he supported the Parliamentarian cause writing prose in praise of Oliver Cromwell and all that he stood for.

A group rowing over to the area near to Milton's Temple. Amazingly, there are nineteen people in this boat which was probably rowed over from Plymouth.

The same group, from the early 1900's, showing Milton's Temple in the background. The man on the left is dressed in a First World War uniform.

The temple as it is today, tucked away in a corner above the duck pond. It looks a bit worse for wear but is still an interesting feature of the gardens.

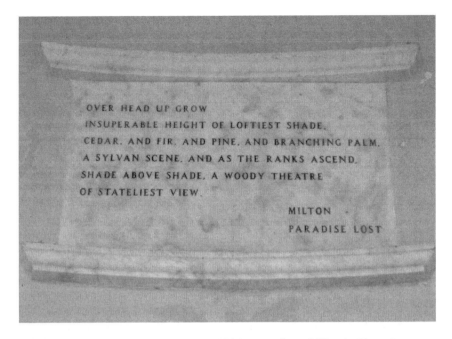

OVER HEAD UP GROW
INSUPERABLE HEIGHT OF LOFTIEST SHADE,
CEDAR. AND FIR. AND PINE. AND BRANCHING PALM.
A SYLVAN SCENE. AND AS THE RANKS ASCEND.
SHADE ABOVE SHADE, A WOODY THEATRE
OF STATELIEST VIEW.

MILTON
PARADISE LOST

The Literary Journal, published in 1821, mentions Milton's Temple:
'In the amphitheatre at Mount Edgcumbe, is erected a small
Grecian temple, in which is placed a bust of Milton, with an
inscription from 'Paradise Lost,' which one could almost imagine
was written on this very spot, every part of the scene so well
agreeing:
'Over head up grow
Insuperable height of loftiest shade,
Cedar and fir, and pine and branching palm.
A sylvan scene.
And as the ranks ascend,
Shade over shade, a woody theatre of stateliest view.
Milton -
Paradise Lost.'

A view looking towards Barn Pool from Milton's Temple. The Garden Battery can be seen in the background.

Fifteen

The People

Mount Edgcumbe and its gardens became famous throughout the 1700s and from 1809, guide books were produced for anyone who wished to visit. At the time, the grounds were open on a Monday.

These photos from the early 1900s show people rowing to the park and enjoying their days picnicing or swimming near to their boats.
The gardens proved very popular during the Victorian and Edwardian period.
In the Tourist's Guide to South Devon : Rail, Road, River and Moor, published in 1883, it said that, **'the Earl of Mount Edgcumbe opens the Park to the public every Wednesday'**. By 1908, the South Devon and South Cornwall Guide stated that, **'Mount Edgcumbe is open to the public on the first Saturday in the month, from whatever point in the Three Towns the Sound can be crossed'**.

A group of ladies who have probably rowed over from Plymouth for the day. Drake's Island and Plymouth can be seen in the background.

Here's the same group, shown earlier by Milton's Temple, enjoying the cool waters. The First World War soldier can be seen sat on the boat.

Here's the same people again and some of the group are enjoying a swim. Little has changed in this area in the time that has passed since.

This photo from the Earl of Mount Edgcumbe Collection, shows the staff of Mount Edgcumbe in 1935 taking a trip in a boat. The estate can be seen in the background.

A small boy is helped over a style by his mother.

This photo shows people dancing at Mount Edgcumbe in the early 1900s. They all have their best clothes on and the ladies all have fancy hats.

This photo seems to show a prize giving event. In the centre of the picture is an old sea captain.

Here, military men mingle amongst the crowd. A refreshment tent on the left has provided tea and sandwiches for the visitors.

There are lots of military men and sailors in this gathering. All these photos of entertainment at Mount Edgcumbe appear to have been taken on the same day.

Written on these two photos was the title 'Kiss in the Ring'. The two photos seem to show a social event and military personnel, including sailors, can be seen in the background.

Two lovely old photos showing the wishing well folly in the early 1900s. Not much has changed in over 100 years.

Sixteen

The Edgcumbe Family

The family history of the Edgcumbes may appear confusing as there are many Richards and Piers and sometimes Piers is referred to as Pears or Peter. The spelling of the surname also varies quite a lot. When William Edgcumbe (William de Eggecombe) married Hilaria in 1352, when Edward III was king, they set up home at Cotehele. Hilaria was the heiress of William de Cotehele and inherited the estate. When William Edgcumbe died in 1380, they had two sons, Peter and William. Hilaria married for a second time to William Fleete. William's son, also William was an MP in the time of King Henry who granted William custody of the lead and silver mines in Devon. William had a son, Peter, who married Elizabeth the daughter of Richard Holland. Peter was the father of Sir Richard Edgcumbe (d. 1489).

Sir Richard Edgcumbe (d. 1489)
Richard Edgcumbe was born at Cotehele, the family's ancestral home, the eldest son of Piers (Peter) Edgcumbe and Elizabeth.
He was the member of parliament for Tavistock in 1467 and he took part in the Duke of Buckingham's rebellion to dethrone Richard III in 1484. When it failed, Richard Edgcumbe became a marked man and a

warrant for his arrest was issued. He was forced to flee and this is recorded in the 1600s by historian Thomas Fuller (1608-1661):

'He was so hotly pursued and narrowly searched for, that he was forced to hide himself in his thick woods at Cuttail (Cotehele), in Cornwall. Here extremity taught him a sudden policy, to put a stone in his cap and tumble the same into the water, whilst those rangers were fast at his heels; who, looking down after the noise, and seeing his cap swinging thereon, supposed that he had desperately drowned himself; and, deluded by this honest fraud, gave over their further pursuit, leaving him at liberty to shift over into Britain (Brittany).'

In France, Richard joined forces with Henry Tudor and accompanied him back to England

Richard Edgcumbe fought together with Henry Tudor, then the Earl of Richmond, at the Battle Of Bosworth and was rewarded for his loyalty. When Richard III fell in battle, Richard Edgcumbe was knighted on the field. He married Joan, the daughter of an important local family, the Tremaynes of Collacombe. He fathered five children.

In 1485, Richard began to remodel the house at Cotehele, which was originally built in the 1200s. When Richard died four years later, the house renovation was completed by his eldest son, Piers. Richard died at Morlaix, while on a diplomatic mission for the King to Brittany. He was later buried there.

Sir Piers Edgcumbe (1472-1539)

When Piers Edgcumbe married Joan Durnford, a 19 year old widow, she brought to her husband land on both sides of the River Tamar. The Edgcumbes were already a wealthy family and the land from the dowry included Stonehouse and what would later become Mount Edgcumbe. With his inheritance, he fortified the town wall near to his Manor House at Stonehouse and also completed the building work at Cotehele which included the hall, parlour and solar. The solar was a room used in medieval times where members of the household, usually the head, would spend time alone away from the hustle and bustle of the main house.

Piers was Sheriff of Devon on several occasions. He was a loyal subject to both Henry VII and Henry VIII. For his services at the battle of Spurs in 1513, he was made Knight-banneret . A Knight banneret was a nobleman who led a company of troops in battle under his own banner. In 1515, Piers was the first Edgcumbe to empark deer on the land that later became Mount Edgcumbe.

Sir Richard Edgcumbe (1499-1562)

Piers son, Richard was born in 1499 and was responsible for building the house at Mount Edgcumbe between 1547 and 1550. It was believed that the house was called 'Mount' Edgcumbe because of the grand manor house that lay opposite called Mount Wise which belonged to the Wise family.

Richard married Elizabeth, the daughter of Sir John Arundell, in 1516. In 1535, he married for a second time to another Elizabeth, the daughter of John Tregian. A third marriage saw him wed to Winifred, the daughter of Sir William Essex.

He became a knight in 1537 and he was Sheriff of Devon between 1543 and 1544. In 1557, he was also Commissioner of the Muster for Cornwall.

The Gentleman's Magazine, published in 1853, mentioned Sir Richard Edgcumbe's generosity:

'Sir Richard Edgcumbe was a man of an enlarged charity, and of a most bountiful spirit; and greatly was it exercised. The destruction of the monasteries had proved fatal to many of the old, the sick, and the helpless, who received their daily support from the monks; and it was long before relief could be organised and formed into anything like a system in the reign of Elizabeth, when England became blessed with so truly Christian an institution as that of the poor law. In Sir Richard's time beggars were almost innumerable throughout the land; and whilst many were rogues and cheats, not a few were objects of real charity. Sir Richard made it a point of duty to relieve all he met, and, consequently, he never stirred out but he met beggars of all ages, kinds, descriptions, and degrees. On one occasion he gave one of these a gold piece of ten instead of a tester, and the poor man, seeing the error, came crouching to him, offering to return it, whereupon Sir Richard, loath to have his alms known, would not so much as hear the poor fellow, but huffed him with 'Away, knave!' this circumstance his good old biographer remarks, " This beggar, for his truth, in my judgment, deserved to possess the hoarded treasures of many a *covetous gruff;* and the knight, for his liberality, was worthy to find the heavenly treasure.'

Richard lived through the turbulent religious changes of the times with the persecution of Catholics and Protestants and the establishment of the Church of England. Richard died in the reign of Elizabeth I.

Sir Piers Edgcumbe (1536-1607)

Born at Cotehele Manor in 1536, Piers was the eldest son of Sir Richard Edgcumbe. He married Margaret Luttrell in 1555. Margaret Luttrell's mother was a descendant of Edward I and a second cousin to both Catherine Howard and Anne Boleyn. They had nine children together and one of their daughters, Margaret, was a maid of honour to Queen Elizabeth I and later married Sir Edward Denny who was the Queen's private messenger.

Piers invested his money in privateering and mining, not always to great success. A privateer was someone who, using their own ship and, with their country's blessing, attacked foreign ships and seized their cargo. In many ways, privateers were just legalised pirates. It made some men very wealthy and Piers would have associated with the sea farers and privateers of the day such as Sir Francis Drake, Sir Walter Raleigh and Sir Charles Howard. The pilchard cellars were built at Cawsand during Piers' lifetime. Piers died in 1607 and his son, also called Piers, inherited the estates.

Sir Richard de Cotehele (1563-1638)

When his brother, Piers, died Richard inherited the Edgcumbe estate. Richard was knighted just before the coronation of James I. He was married twice. He married his first wife, Anne Cary, in 1602 but she unfortunately died in 1607. He married again in 1608 to Mary Coteel, whose father was the wealthy Flemish merchant, Sir Thomas Coteel. Marriage, again, improved the Edgcumbes fortune and this allowed Richard to build the north west tower on Cotehele House. Richard died in 1638.

Colonel Piers Edgcumbe (1610-1667)

Colonel Piers Edgcumbe was also an MP. He married Mary Glanville, the daughter of Sir John Glanville, in 1636. They had one son, Richard (1640-1688). Piers was a supporter of the Royalist cause during the Civil War. The animosity against Piers from the Parliamentarians was such that Sir Alexander Carew of Antony in Cornwall was tried and beheaded just because he had corresponded with the Colonel during the Civil War years. Piers moved to Cotehele so he was further away from the strong Parliamentarian force based just across the water in Plymouth. Millbrook and Mount Edgcumbe were attacked several times and parts of the house were set on fire.

Although Piers was a staunch Royalist, he eventually capitulated to Sir Thomas Fairfax, the Parliamentarian leader. This allowed him to keep his estates intact.

After the restoration of royalty, with the crowning of Charles II in 1661, many Royalist exiles were rewarded for their efforts during the Civil War. Piers made improvements to the grounds at Mount Edgcumbe and a royal licence allowed him to block off the road from Cremyll Passage to Millbrook in 1664 so that the house could be enlarged. A new road was built to replace the old one.

Sir Richard Edgcumbe (1640-1688)

When the Monarchy was restored and Charles II took the throne, Richard was knighted. He married Lady Anne Montagu, the daughter of the Earl of Sandwich, in 1671 and they had two sons, Piers (1676-1694) and Richard (1680-1758). In 1676, Richard was made a Fellow of the Royal Society. The Society's full name was, 'The Royal Society of London for the Improvement of Natural Knowledge' and it was founded in 1660 just a few months after the restoration of Charles II.

Many well-known people visited Richard at Mount Edgcumbe including Charles II and Samuel Pepys. Richard carried on with the renovations to the house started by his father. A new entrance was built and new woods and gardens were laid out. Piers died prematurely at 18 but he outlived Sir Richard. He would have been a boy of 6 when Sir Richard died and the estate eventually passed to his brother, Richard.

Richard, 1st Baron of Edgcumbe (1680-1758)

In 1702, Richard was the Member of Parliament for Plympton Erle, Lostwithiel and St Germans. He also served as Lord of the Treasury and was Paymaster-General for Ireland from 1724 until 1742 when he became the first Baron Edgcumbe. He married Matilda Furnese in 1715. They had two sons, Richard, the 2nd Baron (1716-1761) and George, the 3rd Baron (1720-1795). Richard and Matilda, with their head gardener, Thomas Hull, developed ideas for the gardens which would later, after Matilda's death, include the building of the Folly in 1747 and Milton's Temple in 1755. Matilda died in 1721, a year after George's birth.

When Richard retired from politics in 1742, many of the ideas to alter the garden took place and this work was continued by Richard's sons. Richard lived a very long life, dying in his late nineties. In his time, he saw the reign of six monarchs. He became Chancellor of the Duchy of Lancaster from 1743 until he died in 1758.

The Earl of Mount Edgcumbe Collection

Richard, 2nd Baron of Edgcumbe (1716-1761)

When his father died, Richard inherited the estate but died himself, just three years later.

Richard was a friend of Horace Walpole and part of the Strawberry Hill (Walpole's home) set. He was a known gambler and reports say that he lost 20 guineas daily at White's, a London gentlemen's club that was established in 1693. When he was young, his Grand Tour of Europe was extended by seven years to keep him out of trouble. Henry Pelham, the Prime Minister between 1743 and 1754, paid Richard a secret Service Pension of £500. In 1752, unhappy with relying on Government charity, Richard requested that Pelham give him employment rather than a pension. His request failed but he was eventually made Lord of Trade in 1754. The following year, he was made a Lord of the Admiralty before becoming Comptroller of the Household and Mayor of Lostwithiel in 1756. He was appointed Lord Lieutenant of Cornwall in 1759.

Henrietta Edgcumbe

When Richard died, he was unmarried. However, he fathered four
children with his mistress, Ann Franks Day.
One of his children, Henrietta, married Charles de Prades Lavalette in
1770. The above picture of Henrietta is painted by Joshua Reynolds
and the receipt for the picture says that she is the daughter of Admiral
George Edgcumbe (1721-1795) which might suggest that George
brought her up as his own after Richard's death.

George, 1st Earl (1721-1795)

George was born in 1721 and was the brother of Richard, the 2nd Baron. He was not expected to inherit the estates so joined the Royal Navy. He was quickly promoted from midshipman. He was commissioned a Lieutenant in 1739 and became a Captain in 1744. He served under Edward Hawke and Admiral Edward Boscawen. He married Emma Gilbert in 1761. She was the daughter of John Gilbert, the Archbishop of York.

In 1762, he was promoted to Rear Admiral. Captain Cook and Sir Joseph Banks visited George at Mount Edgcumbe. Cook would later name several places in New Zealand and Australia after Edgcumbe. George became the first Earl of Mount Edgcumbe in 1789. In 1799, the French tried to invade England and part of the French and Spanish fleet sailed into Cawsand Bay. Because fortifications had to be built quickly at Cremyll and Maker, over one hundred ancient trees were cut down on the estate. George's reward for the loss of the trees was that he was made a Viscount when King George III visited in 1781. He became an Earl in 1789.

Richard, 2nd Earl (1764-1839)

Richard was the only child of George, the 1st Earl. He was said to be far less serious than his father. He was an amateur actor and a musician. He wrote the book, 'Musical Reminiscences of the Earl of Mount Edgcumbe' which listed every opera he had heard between 1773 and 1823. His early life included a Grand Tour which included Italy.

He was MP for Lostwithiel and Fowey and later became Lord Lieutenant of Cornwall. Before he became Earl of Mount Edgcumbe in 1795, he was Viscount Valletort.

Richard married Lady Sophia Hobart (1768-1806) in 1789. Her dowry included land at Bere Alston. Their children included William Richard (1794-1818), Ernest Augustus (1797-1861), Lady Emma Sophia (1791-1872) and George Edgcumbe (1800-1882). The Italian and French Gardens were laid out during Richard's time as well as Fern Dell. There were also new drives and plantations created.

Ernest Augustus, the 3rd Earl, pictured in 1855.

Ernest Augustus, 3rd Earl (1797-1861)

Ernest Augustus was an officer in the footguards and saw action during the Waterloo Campaign of 1815.

In 1831, he married Caroline Augusta Fielding (1808-1881) the daughter of the late Admiral Fielding. They had two children, William Henry (1832-1917) and Lady Ernestine Emma Horatia (1843-1925). Ernest was an aid-de-camp to King William IV and also to Queen Victoria and was Colonel of the Cornwall Militia.

In 1850, a book written by the Earl entitled, 'Extracts from a Journal kept during the commencement of the Revolution at Palermo in the year 1848' was published by James Ridgway of Piccadilly. The book referred to the rebelling of Palermo in 1848 against the Neapolitan crown. This continued until May 1849.

In 1855, the Winter Villa was built at Stonehouse and was seen as a more comfortable and suitable dwelling for Ernest who was now in bad health. The house had fifty rooms but was little used after Ernest's death. It was sited where Nazereth House stands today.

William Edgcumbe, the 4th Earl (1832-1917).

William Henry, 4th Earl (1832-1917)

William was the son of Ernest. He married Lady Katherine Hamilton, the daughter of James Hamilton, the 1st Duke of Abercorn, in 1858. He travelled abroad with the Prince of Wales. Katherine died in 1874. He was the first Chairman of the Cornwall County Council in 1888. In the same year his book, 'The Records of the Mount Edgcumbe Family' was published. This proved to be an invaluable source of information after the bombing of the house in 1941 as many records were lost. William married again, this time to his first cousin, Caroline Edgcumbe in 1906. With Katherine, he had a son, Piers who later became the 5th Earl.

A carte de vista of Lady Katherine, Countess of Mount Edgcumbe.

This picture of the Earl and Countess of Mount Edgcumbe was featured in The Bystander of 19th August 1905 and shows them visiting Cotehele. The caption under the headline, **'Lord of a Lordly House'** read:

'The Earl and Countess of Mount Edgcumbe with a favourite dog, Pepper, at the doorway of their medieval home which came to the family about the year 1353 when Hilaria of Cotehele married an Edgcumbe of Edgcumbe. Cotehele is one of the finest examples of medieval domestic architecture in the country, and a place of many interesting memories, as well as a treasure-house of beautiful things. The Earl is Lord-Lieutenant of the County of Cornwall.'

The Bystander, was a weekly illustrated magazine featuring articles on travel, literature, locomotion, fox hunting and social history.

The Earl at the time the picture was taken would have been William Henry Edgcumbe who was born in 1832. He was the 4th Earl.

There is a Pepper, the name of the dog featured on the previous page, buried at Fern Dell which shows that he died in 1920. Presumably, it is the same dog, so it would have had quite a long life.

Piers Alexander, 5th Earl (1865-1944)

Piers married Lady Edith Villiers (1879-1935) in 1911. They had no children and she died in 1935. With Piers, the direct descendancy of the Edgcumbe family came to an end as he had no heir. Interestingly, Lady Edith Villiers, who was born in 1879, was a descendant of William the Conqueror. She was the daughter of Sir Edward Hyde illiers (1846-1914) who was the 5th Earl of Clarendon.

Piers fought in both the Boer War and the First World War. He lived his final two years at Cotehele after his ancestral home at Mount Edgcumbe was bombed during the Second World War. The title then passed to Kenelm who was Pier's second cousin.

Kenelm, 6th Earl (1873-1965)

When he was 71, Kenelm became the 6th Earl of Edgcumbe.

He married Lilian Arkwright in 1906 and he tragically lost his only son, Piers, when he was killed in battle near Dunkirk in 1940. Kenelm was a respected electrical engineer and he wrote the book, 'Industrial Electrical Measuring Instruments', which was published in 1918. He was the President of the Institution of Electrical Engineers.

After the war, Kenelm persuaded the government to take Cotehele in lieu of death duties in 1947 and the ancestral home was handed over to the National Trust. Mount Edgcumbe House had been left a ruin after the bombing of 1941 and Kenelm lived in the stable block from where he and his wife oversaw the restoration of the house.

Lilian, died in 1964 and Kenelm died the following year, aged 92.

Edward Piers, 7th Earl (1903-1982)

When Kenelm died childless in 1965, the family title and estate passed to a distant cousin in New Zealand. Edward Piers farmed sheep in his native country but upon his inheritance, he moved and settled in Cornwall with his wife, Effie.

In 1971, Mount Edgcumbe House and the park were sold jointly to Cornwall County Council and Plymouth City Council. The Earl and his wife continued to live in the house and, during the Summer months, it was open to the public on two days a week.

Robert Charles, 8th Earl (b 1939)

Robert Charles, the current Earl, is also a New Zealander and is a nephew of Edward Piers. His father was George Aubrey Valletort (1907-1977). He married Joan Ivy Wall in 1960 and they have five girls. When they first moved to Cornwall from New Zealand on inheriting the title, they lived at Mount Edgcumbe House until the lease was relinquished in 1987. In 1988, they were divorced and Robert later remarried.

The Earl now lives at Empacombe. In lieu of taxes, the family possessions were given to the Museum and Galleries Commission on the condition that they stay within the house.

After over 400 years in the Edgcumbe family, the house and estate, including Cotehele, was lost due to death duties and taxes.

There are variations to the Coat of Arms for the Barons, Viscounts and Earls of Mount Edgcumbe but this one comes from Catton's English Peerage of 1790 and features a baronial coronet.

The motto reads, 'Au Plesire Fort De Dieu' which translates to, 'At the Almighty disposal of God'. There are variations of the motto and different spellings. The shield shows three boars heads with another boar above a crown. Either side stand two greyhounds.

Seventeen

The Folly

The Folly was built in 1747 and replaced an Obelisk which had stood on the site previously. It was built by using medieval stone from the churches of St George and St Lawrence which once stood in Stonehouse. The same stone was used to build the Picklecombe Seat further along the coast. Part of the seat features a Medieval doorway. The church of St Lawrence was removed to make way for the Royal William Victualling Yard. The Folly was known as 'The Ruins' for many years. Parts of the old Stonehouse Barrier Gates were also said to have been used. As Stonehouse was never a walled town, it is thought that these came from the Abbey or Manor House.

The Pall Mall Magazine, published in 1897, said:
'The ruin was constructed from the remains of a fallen obelisk and some old granite-work.'
This would suggest that the obelisk had collapsed sometime before the building of the folly in 1747. If parts were used within the construction

of the folly then the obelisk erected on Obelisk Hill at Cremyll can't be the complete obelisk that stood where the folly now stands.

An artist painting the scene at the end of the 1800's wrote that the Earl of Edgcumbe had his workers build one folly, had it blown up, didn't like the result and had it built and blown up again to get the result we see today.

The Folly couldn't have pleased everyone and within the pages of A Guide to the Coast of Devon and Cornwall, published in 1859, it says:

'The grounds still are very attractive, but disfigured by silly artificial ruins.'

Also, in Black's Guide to Devonshire, published in 1864, it states:

'Of the mimic ruins scattered through the grounds it is best to take no heed. They are but sorry accessories to a scene which nature has so bounteously enriched.'

Perhaps these comments are unfair but maybe, at the time, they were seen by the Edgcumbes, as they are today, as adding interest to the impressive landscape. The Folly was built at a time when such buildings were fashionable.

Three women make their way up the steep path towards the folly. There is another group of people behind them at the bottom of the path. They were probably heading towards the tea house at Lady Emma's Cottage.

This photo taken in 1885 shows the ivy covered Folly, on the right, and Drake's Island and Plymouth in the background.

A daytrip to the Folly in 1928. A boy on the left is exploring the Folly while this photo is being taken. The man in the middle is holding an old Kodak Box Brownie camera so there would have been more photos of the trip. I wonder if the pictures still survive?

An Autumn shot, with leaves on the ground, showing the path leading upwards towards the Folly. This view is almost exactly the same as Victorian visitors would have seen it.

The Folly silhouetted against an evening sky.

Looking through a window of the Folly towards the park and Plymouth beyond.

Eighteen.

Lady Emma's Cottage

The original cottage was built in Beechwood in 1760 and it burned down in 1880. It was rebuilt as Lady Emma's Cottage in 1882. The plans for the cottage were drawn up by William Morris, the interior designer. At the time, the Edgcumbe family insisted that the cottage was for estate workers only and could only be occupied by men. The cottage was named after Lady Emma Edgcumbe, who was the daughter of the Second Earl of Mount Edgcumbe. The rebuilt building was still known as Beechwood Cottage for many years. During Victorian times, it became a very popular tea room for the many people who visited the Mount Edgcumbe Estate.

The 1881 Census shows that a George Wilson, aged 49, lived at Lady Emma's cottage with his wife, the aptly named, Emma. George was employed as a house steward on the estate.

However, the 1891 census refers to the building again as Beechwood Cottage. During that time, a Richard Ryder, aged 49, lived there with his wife and five children. Richard worked as a gardener's labourer. Also living there at the same time was a William Strike, aged 59, together with his wife and his three children. William was employed as a wheelwright. During the 1950s, it was home to Mr Burgess, the chauffeur. Other occupants of the house included Mr and Mrs Chamberlain. Mr Chamberlain was the carter on the estate.

Lady Emma Edgcumbe was born in 1791 and married Sir John Cust, who was the 1st Earl of Brownlow, in 1828. She was his third wife and they had no children together although Sir John had five children from previous marriages. Emma held the position of Lady of the Bedchamber to the Queen Consort, Adelaide, until 1849. She also wrote a book called,

'Reminiscences Of A Septuagenarian From 1802 To 1815'. Emma Place in Stonehouse was named after her and Caroline Place was named after her sister. Emma died in 1878 and is remembered by some, probably wrongly, connected to the strange tale, previously mentioned, of the sexton who stole her rings.

Beechwood Cottage before the fire.

Lady Emma (1791-1872) shouldn't be confused with the earlier Emma Gilbert (1729-1807) who was married to George Edgcumbe (1721-1795), the 1st Earl.

Two Victorian boys sit on the banks by the rebuilt Lady Emma's Cottage. During the time of this picture, the house was a very popular tea room and garden.

A photo showing the many visitors enjoying tea at the house in the early 1900s. More visitors can be seen heading towards the teahouse on the path on the right of the picture.

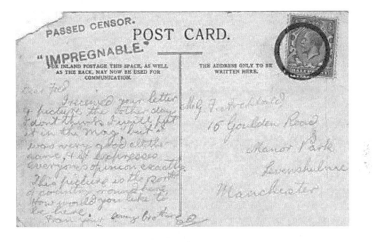

Here's the reverse of a postcard that features Beechwood Cottage on the front. What's interesting is that the card bears the hand stamp, 'Passed Censor - Impregnable'. This must have been sent from someone serving on HMS Impregnable, which in the early 1900s was moored off Cremyll. It reads, 'Dear Fred, I received your letter and picture the other day. I don't think I will put it in the 'mag' but it was very good all the same, and it expresses everyone's opinion exactly. This picture is the sort of country around here. How would you like to be here? From your loving brother, Edward. The stamp features George V so this must have been posted during or after 1910.

This photo from the Earl of Mount Edgcumbe Collection shows the cottage as it was in the 1960s.

Nineteen

The Deer Park

In 1515, Sir Piers Edgcumbe was given permission by King Henry VIII to keep deer and the deer park was formed soon after. During the reign of Henry VIII, there was a deer park attached to the Durnford manor house in Stonehouse. It is thought that Piers Edgcumbe probably took deer from this stock to start his new herd. At one time, their ancestors would have roamed Stonehouse Park which would have been found where the western end of Union Street is today. The descendants of the original deer can still be seen roaming the Edgcumbe Estate today and are thought to be one of the oldest strains of deer in the country.
During the Second World War, the Deer Park was used as an anti-aircraft and barrage balloon site.

A photo from the 1870s showing the deer park near to the Folly. Within the Grotton Plantation is the Higher Deer house which was once a fodder store for the deer in the park. It was built in the 1800s.

An entry in the National Archives for 25th May 1639 shows, **'Pears Edgecombe of Mt Edgcombe appointed to be master and governor of his game of red deer and venison.'**

Two Victorian ladies, complete with parasols, enjoying a stroll in the deer park. In the background is the dockyard at Devonport.

In The Book of Fair Devon by the United Devon Association, published in 1900, it says:
'One of the finest views from the grounds of Mount Edgcumbe is that from the White Seat at the summit of the deer park. From this point of vantage the towns of Plymouth, Stonehouse and Devonport are spread out like a map and in the extreme distance rise the high range of the Dartmoor Hills.'

An early view looking towards the Garden Battery and Plymouth.

An etching from 1887 showing a hunting party probably shooting pheasants. This view looks very similar today.

An evening shot with deer on the horizon within the park.

The Pall Mall Magazine, published in 1897, mentioned the Deer Park: **'From a ship's deck, the fallow deer can be seen, dotted over the short turf, and, with a good glass, even the multitudinous of rabbits can be discerned - a sight which must have aroused the sporting instincts of generations of middies.'**

The upper part of the Deer Park towards Maker Church. Maker is the Edgcumbes' family church and was built in 1186 and was enlarged in the 1400s. Nearby are the dog kennels which were built in the 1800s. They include runs for five dogs.

Looking from the Deer Park towards the Folly with Plymouth in the background.

An evening shot with the last rays of light hitting the gate. You would think that this gate and fence would be sufficient to keep the deer in one place but they can easily leap over it though they always seem to return to the main part of the Deer Park eventually.

Twenty

Empacombe

John Rudyerd lived at Empacombe in 1706 together with his Eddystone Lighthouse workshop. Rudyerd's lighthouse was built of wood and was completed in 1709. It was the second Eddystone lighthouse to be built. The first, built by Winstanley, was swept away in a storm in 1703. Rudyerd's lighthouse was destroyed by fire in 1755. Rudyerd was a silk merchant who was based in London. Two shipwrights called Smith and Northcutt were employed to help him design the new lighthouse.
From the 1881 census, a George Brighton lived at Empacombe with his daughters, Clara and Emily. He was 60 years old at the time and was employed as head gardener at Mount Edgcumbe. Other people living at Empacombe included George Adams, aged 27, who lived with his wife, Hannah, and daughter, Jessie. He was also employed as a gardener on the Mount Edgcumbe Estate. Charles Penprase also lived at Empacombe in 1881 when he was aged 30 and was an agricultural labourer. His wife Mary, aged 31, and his mother, Ann, aged 68, lived with him. Also in 1881, Samuel Harvey, aged 70, lived at the Empacombe with his family. He was a Land Agent .
There is an Empacombe Battery which was constructed in 1803 and is built of stone. It is also known as the Maker Redoubt No. 6.

The houses close to the harbour. The Cherry Blossom tree on the right is in full bloom in this picture.

A view looking back through the door of the old windmill. The disused mill makes an interesting feature on the landscape.

A photo of the old windmill. The tower is 25 ft tall and the windmill is one of only six remaining in Cornwall. The sails are long gone. It appears in records in 1729 but it may be older than this.

Twenty One

Fort Picklecombe

The original battery at Fort Picklecombe was built of earth in 1849. Between 1864 and 1871, a more substantial building replaced it made of granite with iron shields. It was armed with 42 guns and was one of three main fortifications protecting the Sound.

Picklecombe Fort was commissioned by Lord Palmerston who was the foreign secretary and Prime Minister during the reign of Queen Victoria. Palmerston's forts appeared all over Britain following concerns over the size of the French Navy. They gained the name, Palmerston's Follies and by the time they were completed, the threat had passed. They were said to be the most expensive system of defence structures ever built in Britain during times of peace.

The 1881 census shows Fort Picklecombe occupied by the military and their families. Residents at the time included one Major, four Sergeants, three Corporals, five Bombers, two Trumpeters, fifty seven gunners as well as several wives and children.

The battery in 1905. The Breakwater can be seen out to sea.

The tree-lined avenue leading towards Picklecombe.

Fort Picklecombe was redeveloped into apartments in the 1970s and is now a private establishment that doesn't welcome walkers or visitors. Ramblers might find that the occupants are more defensive than the army that once inhabited the fort. The fort is an interesting feature though and it seems a pity that it is off limits to the general public.

Twenty Two

Kingsand

In 1483, a handful of fishermen lived at Kingsand and Cawsand when Henry VII landed in an abortive attempt to try to overthrow Richard III. The population grew when Plymouth merchants built pilchard cellars along the shore in the time of Elizabeth I. For the next two centuries, smuggling also flourished.

In 1844, the pilchard fishery in both Kingsand and Cawsand employed fifty men.

Up until 1844, Kingsand was still in Devon and a boundary marker between the two counties can still be seen opposite the Halfway Hotel which separated Turk Town (Cawsand) and North Rockers (Kingsand). Horatio Nelson was said to have visited the village and to have dined at the Ship Inn.

Famous residents have included Ann Davison who sailed the Atlantic single-handedly in 1953. Arthur Ransome's daughter Tabitha also lived here. Ransome was famous for writing, 'Swallows and Amazons.'

The Cleave from Kingsand Bay with many small boats on its shore.

The History of Cornwall by Fortescue Hitchins and Samuel Drew, published in 1824, stated:

'Trending Penlee Point,' says Carew, ' you discover Kingsand and Cawsand Bay, an open road, yet sometimes affording succour to the worst of seafarers, as not subject to the controlment of Plymouth forts. The shore is peopled with some dwelling-houses and many cellars, dearly rented for a short usage in saving pilchards; at which time there flocketh a great number of seiners and others depending on their labour. I have heard the inhabitants thereabout report, that the Earl of Richmond, afterwards Henry VII, while he hovered upon the coast, here by stealth refreshed himself; but being advertised of strait watch kept for him at Plymouth, he richly rewarded his host, hied speedily on shipboard, and escaped happily to a better fortune.'

'In 1597, a Spanish ship coming into the bay, while most of the active men were absent at an assize, seized this favourable opportunity to send a party on shore in the dead of night to make preparations for setting the town on fire. To accomplish this, they hung up some barrels of combustible matter to several doors, to which a train was set, that at a given time should take fire, and execute their purpose. Happily however, the design being discovered before the explosion took place, these unwelcome guests were removed, and the Spaniards driven on board their ship. Carew observes, that the contriver of this plot was a Portuguese, who had sailed with Sir John Boroughs, and boasted to have burned his ship. For these two honourable exploits the king of Spain is said to have rewarded him with 200 ducats. Kingsand and Cawsand contain many houses and many inhabitants. About forty years since, smuggling was carried on here to a considerable extent; at which time this place produced some of the most able seamen in the west of England. But of late years, since this contraband traffic has been on the decline, the inhabitants have directed their talents into another channel. Some branches of the Royal Navy riding in this bay during the late war, furnished the industrious with employment in trading to the ships, and supplying their crews with necessaries. This consolidated town lies in a pleasant vale on the margin of the tide. It has many well-built houses; and from those situated on elevated ground, the prospects are extensive, diversified and pleasing. The streets however, are narrow and irregular, and cannot be distinguished for the excellence of their pavement, or extraordinary cleanliness.'

The ruins of the old pilchard cellars can be seen in the background of this photo. Little has changed since this photo was taken.

An old photo showing a group on a daytrip to Kingsand.

People bathing in a saltwater pool. The swimming costumes have certainly changed over the years as too have the fashions.

A boy and his sister on a boat just off the shore. Plymouth can be seen in the background.

A group having a picnic near to the old pilchard cellars. Richard Treville, an Elizabethan merchant, owned fish cellars here and he exported fumados, which were smoked pilchards. These were known as 'fairmaids' to the French and Spanish. Treville Street in Plymouth is named after him.

A boat heading out from the beach at Kingsand perhaps rowing back to Barn Pool at Mount Edgcumbe and then to Plymouth.

This could be a works outing or one of the many church trips that were organised at the time. The people in this picture feature in the picture in the boat on the previous page.

Fort Picklecombe can be seen in the background as a young boy mans the boat while others enjoy a swim.

Twenty Three

Cawsand

Cawsand was perfectly placed for the practice of smuggling. Goods from France such as tobacco, tea and rum were off loaded from incoming ships and taken to shore by longshoremen's boats. Open boats, normally used for seine net fishing to catch pilchards were manned by six-man crews and were well adapted to meet ships to offload goods. They were also able to cross the Channel in these boats and could carry as much as six tons of brandy at a time. Larger boats could carry as much as 800 eight-gallon spirit casks as well as sundry other goods. In 1804, the collector of Customs in Plymouth estimated that over 17,000 casks of wine were smuggled into Cawsand and avoided duty every year. In 1815, fifty boats were involved in the trade. There were many battles between smugglers and revenue men within the bay. In one, in 1788, Henry Carter, who was one of Cornwall's most famous smugglers and who was nicknamed the 'King of Prussia', barely escaped with his life, though he lost his cutter in the fight. Henry Carter's real name was John Carter and he modelled himself on Frederick the Great, the King of Prussia. Carter lived at what is known today as Prussia Cove, originally Porthleah, in West Cornwall and the name has been adopted from his nickname.

When the smuggling trade finally ended, Cawsand men returned to fishing and pilotage.

A young sailor from Cawsand, Lieutenant John Pollard, was a midshipman on the Victory when Nelson was fatally wounded. Although not a well known name now, it was Pollard who shot and killed the enemy sailor who shot Nelson. He was known thereafter as, 'Nelson's Avenger'. However, several other men also claimed to have shot the Frenchman.

In An Authentic Narrative of the Death of Lord Nelson by Sir William Beatty, published in 1807, he wrote:

'There were only two Frenchmen left alive in the mizzen-top of the Redoubtale at the time of his Lordship's being wounded and by the hands of these he fell. At length one of them was killed by a musket ball; and on the others then attempting to make his escape

from the top down the rigging, Mr Pollard (Midshipman) fired his musket at him and shot him in the back when he fell dead from the shrouds on the Redoutable's poop.'

Beatty was the Ship's Surgeon on HMS Victory and his account supports Pollard being the 'avenger'.

Captain Frederick Lewis Maitland sailed from Cawsand Bay on the 24th May, 1815, in command of His Majesty's ship, Bellerophon. Napoleon was defeated at the Battle of Waterloo on the 18th June 1815. With the French army in disarray, coalition forces were able to enter France and restore Louis XVIII to the French throne. Unable to return to France, Napoleon made his way towards America. Maitland intercepted Napoleon at Rochefort and after negotiations, Napoleon surrendered to Maitland on the 15th July 1815.

Maitland refused Napoleon passage to America and took him to England arriving at Torbay on the 24th July where he was ordered to proceed to Plymouth. Napoleon was to spend the last six years of his life in exile, under British supervision, on the island of St Helena.

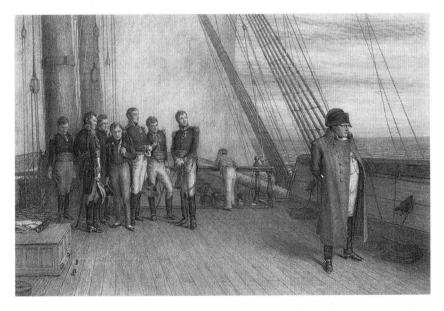

A 19th century engraving of Napoleon on the Bellerophon overlooked by the ship's officers. This engraving was taken from an original painting by Sir William Orchardson (1832-1910) who was a Scottish portraitist who also painted scenes of a historical interest.

Nettleton's Guide of 1829 described Cawsand and Kingsand within its pages:

'This place has partaken largely in the prosperity which the whole neighbourhood owes to the naval establishments in the district. In Carew's time, it consisted of only a few fisherman's huts; it now contains over 300 houses, many of them large and well-built. Its support which, in time of war, was principally derived from the number of ships which resorted to the bay, is now confined to the fisheries, particularly that of pilchards which we regret have been unproductive for many years past. Two dissenting places of worship are well attended by the inhabitants, the respective churches being at a considerable distance. On a rocky eminence which arises near the centre of Cawsand are the vestiges of a fortification at present called 'The Bulwarks'.

During the tremendous storm of 1817, this town sustained very great injury. Some houses on the beach were entirely destroyed by the violence of the waters and there was property lost and destroyed to a considerable amount. It also suffered in the hurricane of November 1824 and January 1828 when the destruction again was very extensive.'

A view looking downwards towards the village. Little has changed over the years.

The West Britton of 27 January 1817 carried details of the great storm of 1817:

'On Sunday last soon after dark, a violent gale of wind came on from the South-East which about midnight increased to one of the most tremendous storms which the oldest inhabitants recollect to have witnessed, being scarcely equalled by that which carried away the Eddystone Light many years ago. Kingsand and Cawsand have suffered considerably; the damage done at these places is estimated at upwards of £5,000. One house, with a man who dwelt in it, was completely swept away. Some of the fish-cellars with nets etc were swept into the ocean. Nearly all the quays for loading limestone etc round the port are either damaged or entirely swept away. Of one lately built by Mr Fuge, which cost upwards of £600, not a stone is left on another.'

On the 28th April 1912, the Titanic survivors were brought back to Millbay Docks, fourteen days after the ship had sank. At 8 am, the SS Lapland moored at Cawsand Bay with the 167 members of the Titanic who hadn't been detained in New York for the American inquiry. Three tenders left Millbay Docks to collect the passengers and the 1,927 sacks of mail that had been scheduled to be carried by the Titanic. The third tender, the Sir Richard Grenville, carrying the survivors, killed time in the Sound while the dock labourers and porters were paid off and escorted out of the dock gates at West Hoe. After midday, the tender was given the all clear and the survivors were allowed to disembark in an air of secrecy. They were then put on a special train from Millbay Docks to Southampton where they arrived at 10.10pm that night.

A group of ladies gathered on the shores of Cawsand in 1921.

The St Georges Road Methodist Club with their boat at Cawsand.
Seventeen members of the crew can be seen in this picture.

The Pennycross Methodist Club in 1924 on Cawsand Beach.

A man and his son sitting on a wall at Cawsand in 1929. The boy has a handful of wild flowers. There are people walking in the field in the background and the sea can also be seen in the distance.

The view of the beach and coast at Cawsand. The view looks towards Penlee Point.

This picture of the Normandie is taken off Cawsand Bay. The Normandie steamed into Plymouth Sound in 1937 after crossing the Atlantic in a record breaking time. The Normandie was the industry's first 1,000 ft ocean liner. Walt Disney was among the many famous passengers who landed at Plymouth. The liner capsized and caught fire in New York while being converted for use in the Second World War.

HMS Alcide P415 in Cawsand Bay in 1947. The P415 was commissioned late in the war (1945) and was an Amphion class submarine built by Vickers-Armstrong.

This photo shows the 17th century Smuggler's Inn in the square at Cawsand. On the wall is a tin sign advertising, 'Lyon's Tea'. For many years, the inn carried the name, 'The Smuggler's Inn' but now it has reverted back to its original name, 'The Cross Keys'.

The view along the beach looking towards Picklecombe Fort in the background. The red rock (rhyolite) is volcanic and trapped air bubbles from eruptions millions of years ago can be seen. The pilchard cellars are built from this material as are many of the houses in Kingsand.

Twenty Four

Queen Adelaide's Grotto and Penlee Point

Duprez's Guide of 1871 states:

'At Penlee Point is the Beacon, a lofty obelisk erected as a landmark for sailors. Here is also a pretty Gothic building called 'Adelaide's Chapel' in honour of the Queen, who during a visit in 1827 made many excursions to the spot.'

The Beacon mention in Duprez's Guide was said to be a Folly Tower which stood above the ridge of Queen Adelaide's Chapel. It was erected by the first Earl so that he could signal to his returning ships. It was considered a security risk and removed during the First World War.

The path leading from Penlee Point. The villages of Cawsand and Kingsand can be seen in the background.

Queen Adelaide (1792-1849) was the wife of William IV (1765-1837).
Adelaide in Australia was named after her in 1836.
Queen Adelaide's Grotto was originally just a cave and was used as a
watch house in the 18th Century. It was enhanced with an arched stone
frontage and became a grotto after Adelaide's visit in 1827. If you didn't
know it was there, it would be easy to miss as it is set down from the
main walking path above.

An old etching showing the grotto, with several men enjoying a picnic
with baskets of food and bottles of wine.

A Victorian lady walks along the road close to Penlee Point. In the
background can be seen the chapel at Rame Head.

A view above the lane at Penlee Point. The steep steps in the picture
were constructed so that the barrel for a 69 ton gun could be delivered
for installation within the Victorian Penlee Battery, which once stood
further up the hill.

A view looking up towards the grotto.

Some of the graffiti on the wall behind the seat within the grotto. Some of it dates back to the 1800s.

A view looking out to sea from inside the grotto. On a sunny day, the water has a Mediterranean look about it with deep blues and greens.

A view from Queen Adelaide's Grotto looking towards Rame Head. The Norman chapel at Rame, built in 1239, can be seen in the background.

Twenty Five

Rame Head

Hermits lived at the ancient chapel of St Michael and kept a light burning to warn ships of the danger of the nearby rocks. The first record of the chapel appears in 1397. By 1425, a licence was granted to hold mass every Monday and at Michaelmass.

By 1488, the men who inhabited the chapel were paid 4d for 'keeping of ye bekying'. They would also report back any news of incoming vessels. In 1588, two watchmen were paid to keep a look out for Spanish vessels after the abortive attempt of the Armada. During the First World War, an anti-submarine gun was mounted on a platform near the chapel and in the Second World War, a concrete gun platform was built and a mobile radar station was located there.

St. Michael the Archangel is known as the patron saint of high and exposed places such as St. Michael's Mount in Marazion and Mont-Saint-Michel, close to Normandy.

Flint tools found in the area date from the Mesolithic period. In the Iron Age, the headland was separated from the mainland by a huge ditch.

In 1882, the chapel was restored by William, the 4th Earl of Edgcumbe.

Two photos showing the same group of picnickers just below Rame Head. They've come prepared with china cups and a wicker food basket. The lady on the left, in the top picture, has hair almost down to her feet.

The same picnickers can be seen in this photo with the chapel in the background.

Rame Head can be seen in the background as children enjoy playing on the beach.

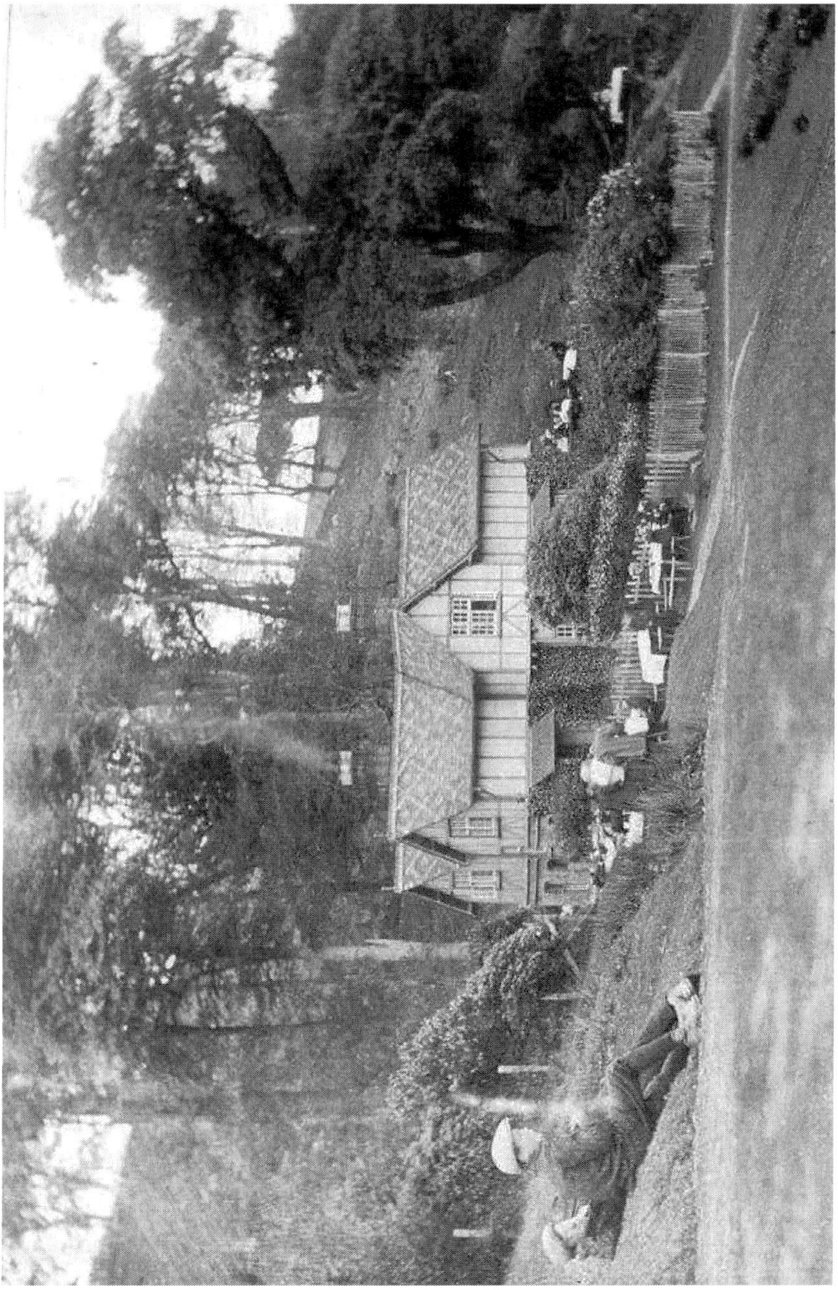

160

By the same author :

St Budeaux

St Budeaux

A history of St Budeaux, Plymouth. Contains over 150 old photos and illustrations.
108 pages.
Price : £9.99.
ISBN-13: 978-0955427763.

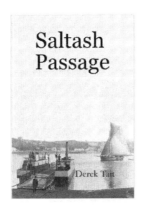

Saltash Passage

A history of Saltash Passage, Plymouth. Contains over 140 old photos and illustrations.
104 pages.
Price : £9.99.
ISBN-13: 978-0955427732.

Plymouth
Hoe

Derek Tait

Plymouth Hoe

A history of Plymouth Hoe. Contains 172 old photos and illustrations.
128 pages.
Price : £9.99.
ISBN : 978-0-9554277-7-0.

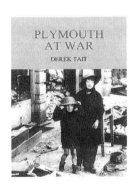

Plymouth at War

A history of Plymouth. Contains 200 old photos and illustrations.
130 pages.
Price : £9.99.
ISBN : 978-0955427787.

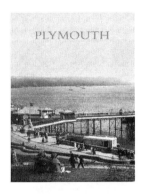

Plymouth

A history of Plymouth. Contains 200 old photos and illustrations.
130 pages.
Price : £9.99.
ISBN : 978-0955427794.

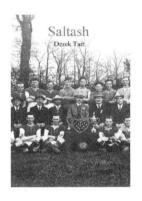

Saltash

A history of Saltash. Contains over 150 old photos and illustrations.
128 pages.
Price : £9.99.
ISBN : 978-0-9560781-0-0.

Sampans, Banyans and Rambutans
A Childhood in Singapore and Malaya

A childhood spent in Singapore and Malaya in the 1960s as part of a Naval family.
104 pages.
Price : £7.99.
ISBN-13: 978-0955427701.

Memories of Singapore and Malaya

Memories of Singapore and Malaya during the 1950s,1960s and 1970s through the eyes of servicemen and their families.
Contains 230 photos.
194 pages.
Price : £9.99.
ISBN-13: 978-0955427756.